MW01620184

BEYOND SURVIVAL

A True Story of an Enduring Spirit

Anita's Story

As told to Karen Cauble

Aardvark Global Publishing
Salt Lake City, Utah
2016

Cover: Graphic art by
Valerie Miller, Studio Services
www.StudioServices-Design.com

Original Design suggested by Gina R. Ford
Flowers: Bravoin, "Colorful Flowers," 10415484.
Dreamstime.com

Chapter images obtained from: www.PublicDomainVectors.org
www.WpClipart.com

ISBN 978-1-4276-9684-7
Aardvark Global Publishing, LLC
Salt Lake City, UT

Print on Demand edition through Kindle Direct Publishing

Also available as Kindle eBook

I want to thank everyone who has encouraged me to write this book and has supported me on this journey. The events shared in the book are based on my memories. Some incidents have official, public documentation to support their occurrence, others are my personal perceptions.

Some names have been changed to respect the wishes and privacy of others. Some of the events described are graphic, but need to be told as they really happened in order for you to possibly understand my experiences.

Forward

We all have a story to tell. As human beings, we make our own personal and individual histories. Our lives are intertwined with the lives of others. I believe we are influenced to some degree by almost everyone we meet. In turn, we also have the opportunity to influence the lives and happiness of others.

Everyone perceives life with their own eyes, influenced by *their* thoughts, opinions, feelings, and history. Experiences can affect their perceptions over time. It is often too easy for others to form opinions about us or judge us. In reality, usually no two experiences are exactly alike, and no one can come close to understanding what another person has gone through unless they have gone down a similar road. To put it another way, people sometimes have to walk through fire to really know how hot it is! To imagine walking in another person's shoes is to open yourself to seeing a different perspective, and to allow for personal growth.

Often, we don't realize how powerful words can be. To think them is one thing, to speak them is another. Words can move us into action. Sometimes those words or actions may not be perceived the way we intended. People may not remember exact words spoken, but they may remember how they felt when they heard them. The consequences of things said may surprise us. I've learned to pause and think before I speak as much as I possibly can.

During my lifetime, I discovered many mysteries about my heritage. I have lived through life-altering events. There were times I wanted to say, "Enough is enough! I want this to stop!" Somehow, I learned how to cope and eventually deal with some of the consequences. It has taken me years to solve some of the unknowns, and to get even a hint at why they took place in my life. As I have recovered from the traumatic events and grown personally, I have come to know that the physical wounds of victims are only superficial. The real wounds are the ones that are unseen.

I'd like to share some of my history with you and tell you what I have learned about my life and the world. This is *my* reality.

I have experienced the journey of LIFE!!!

TABLE OF CONTENTS

BEYOND SURVIVAL

A True Story of an Enduring Spirit

Anita's Story

Introduction

My life's journey has presented me with many challenges. I have learned much through relationships with people, raising children, and working in a variety of jobs. I cared for and protected loved ones and survived events that at times I thought might do me in.

It is important to me that my family have the opportunity to know how I came to be the person I am today. With the encouragement of my husband Jerry, I decided to tackle putting my story in writing. This became another unexpected journey in its own right. Initially, I recorded my memories and comments on a tape recorder and hired a ghost writer to put the information together. I appreciate the work that person did to get me started on this project. Later, I enlisted the help of a friend to edit what had been done so far, and we expanded it significantly. Working together we have been able to find the words and phrases that best express my story and feelings.

We begin my tale with my childhood years, when my life initially appeared normal to me. I was being raised in a traditional Mexican-American family in Northern California. When I was seven years old, I began to feel I didn't really *fit* in the family. The feeling came to me one day as I was sitting on the hood of my dad's 1952 Chevy. I sensed I didn't belong. I didn't know why, I just felt it strongly enough to believe it. I was convinced that, somehow, I belonged to another family. I just *knew* it! I suspected that the people I was living with, Ruth and Joseph, the people I knew as "Mom and Dad," were *not* my birth parents. They were very loving parents and always treated me well. Other adults in the family, however, treated me very differently from the other children. They made snide remarks, even telling me I was ugly and would never find a man who would want me. As a child, I certainly didn't understand what they meant by that, but I knew it was not a nice thing to say. Sometimes they referred to me as a spoiled little brat who would never amount to anything. When we went to the family gathering every Christmas Eve, I had to just sit back and watch as my cousins received gifts from the "Santa" who was greeting them with gifts and cajoling. There was never anything for me. I think the unkind words had an impact on me for years. I struggled with a lack of self-confidence, and I feel those childhood impressions may have influenced some of my decisions as a teenager and young adult.

As an adult, one day I was going through papers and happened to find my birth certificate. I noticed that the signature in the place for Name of Mother did not match my mother's handwriting. I pulled out my brother Rocky's birth certificate to compare the signatures. They did *not* match.

I also compared the ages stated for Ruth and Joseph on both certificates. His stated our mother was twenty-one years old in 1933. The date on *my* certificate in 1952 stated she was twenty-nine years old. How could that be possible? There were nineteen years between 1933 and 1952, and Rocky *was* nineteen years older than me, yet the certificates indicated Mom had only aged eight years in between our births? Obviously, something was not right.

Joseph, born in 1894, was stated as being fifty when I was born. The numbers didn't add up. He was actually fifty-eight in 1952 when I was born. This was getting VERY interesting. It sparked my interest even more to find out more about my heritage. Over the years, every time I thought I had a clue, it turned out to be a dead end or brought up more questions. Believe me; it has turned into quite an adventure trying to sort fact from fiction!

During this writing process, I have had to essentially relive in my mind and soul the events of my past. There have been moments of joy and humor as I recalled some situations, but the images of the darker, more traumatic moments were so vivid they were very hard to face again. There were times I had to stop because I became very anxious. I would physically shake, and tears would stream down my cheeks. Reliving those painful moments from my past, I realized how much emotion I had bottled up over the years and shoved to the back of my mind where I hoped I would *not* have to think about or feel those events again. Passing through my teenage years and into my thirties, I blocked emotions in order to cope with the acts of daily living. I had no time or energy to "feel." I took all my responsibilities seriously, and would do whatever it took to fulfill them. I had to focus on survival. Most of the time, it was all I could do to get through each day.

I eventually escaped the most dangerous situations I found myself in, and met a wonderful man to whom I have been happily married for over thirty years. His love and support, combined with my spirit and tenacity, have allowed me to become more self-confident, and to accomplish more than I ever thought possible for me. Sometimes I look back at all that has happened in my life and am amazed that I survived! Certain events occurring over the past three decades have caused emotions to surface that I had previously blocked. I have had to learn to deal with them. While at times very painful, I believe the journey of writing this book has been a healing adventure.

In my mind, this book will have two functions. One is to enlighten my family, the other is to share my experiences with people who have had, or are dealing with, similar situations. I want them to see that they are not alone. I sincerely hope they will seek support and gain the strength and courage to escape possibly dangerous, life threatening circumstances. Through my own experience, I know that it *is* possible to live through traumatic events, move forward, and find true happiness.

1. The Journey Begins

My story began in San Francisco, California, where I was born in the winter of 1952. My parents Ruth and Joseph, my brother Rocky, and I lived in San Francisco until I was five years old, at which time we moved to a rural area of East San Jose known back then as a barrio. For those of you unfamiliar with that term, a barrio is one or more blocks of houses that form a territorial unit. This barrio was a rough area because of gang activity. It was a difficult place to start school, and even more difficult to establish friendships. The only way I could invite a girlfriend to my house was to meet her on "neutral territory," like the corner store. I'd walk her into the neighborhood and, of course, later walk her out. The fact that we lived on a dead-end street with an open field behind it made it even more intimidating. The neighborhood was known as Sal se puede, which translated means "Get out if you can."

Dad bought the house in San Jose for five hundred dollars. It originally had three rooms: one bedroom, a living room, and the kitchen. I still recall that the bedroom I shared with Rocky had a barn door to enter the room. Mom and Dad slept in the living room. As I look back now, I realize that they sacrificed their privacy so that Rocky and I could have our own room. Soon after we moved in, Dad built the indoor bathroom, which was large enough to also store the wringer-washer. When Mom was doing the laundry, she put the hose into the bathtub to drain the water out. I think Dad was pretty clever to build the room with that in mind!

When the indoor bathroom was complete, he removed the outhouse that was in the back yard. Then he built an addition on the house: a dining room and two extra rooms. One was a bedroom for Mom and Dad, and the other was for Mom's stepfather to live in. It was a large room, so half of it was used to store the three galvanized garbage cans that contained our food staples: flour, pinto beans, and rice. The big backyard had plenty of space to grow fresh vegetables, and we had several fruit trees. The detached garage had a storage room for the canned goods that Mom put up every year. She taught me how to can fruits, make tortillas and tamales, and cook other foods. No matter how little money we had, we always had enough to eat.

Dad wanted everything just right. At that time, only stores had picture windows, so when he installed a large picture window in our living room, our house was one of the more modern homes on the block. We were also lucky enough to have one of the first color televisions in the neighborhood. When I was young, one of my favorite shows was "The Mickey Mouse Club." Later on, it was "Dick Clark's American Bandstand," then "Shindig," another popular music and dance show. Rocky especially loved sitting in front of the TV – in fact, he still does. He learned a lot over the years from television programs. With his learning difficulties, it became a good teaching tool for him. "The Price is Right" helped him learn numbers, and "Queen for a Day" educated him on household chores and appliances. "The Lawrence Welk Show" taught us both about music. Rocky knows so much trivia now; just ask him who starred in one of the old movies. He can tell you the names of most of the celebrities!

The garage had a room that became my playhouse. It had an old-fashioned radio and a table with chairs. It was just like my own miniature house! I had one of the first Chatty Cathy dolls. My girlfriends would come over and we'd play house there. Many times we dressed up as little princesses, putting on Mom's dresses and hiking them up in back to make a train. Our plastic hair bands were magically transformed into crowns or tiaras.

Over the years we had approximately one hundred cats in our backyard. Living out in the country, we didn't have to buy cat food for them, but we did put our table scraps out for them. One of them would ride in the basket on my bike when I went to the grocery store. We called another one who seemed to be a "leader," Grandma. The time one kitten I was especially attached to died, I held a funeral and we buried her in the back yard, complete with a little church-type ceremony.

We owned a Model T at that time, but my dad wanted a Cadillac, so he went out and bought it. Mom got very mad at him, probably because it was expensive, so he ended up returning it. He retaliated by buying a Nash Rambler, a car she really disliked. Later, around 1959, he bought a top-of-the-line, beautiful, black Imperial, complete with the latest perks, like push button windows and other new features of the times. The next purchase was a little white Chrysler Plymouth, followed by a 1952 Chevy. Dad loved his cars! We kept the Chevy until I was about 14 years old.

Mom didn't drive because she hadn't gotten a driver's license, but I remember the one time she drove the Chevy. Dad had gone to the wrestling matches in downtown San Jose. Usually, Mom went to the movies on wrestling days, but this Wednesday she didn't want to see the film that was playing. As soon as Dad left, she got Rocky and me into the car, and she got behind the steering wheel. She was only 4'11", so she could barely see over the dash and had to look through the opening of the steering wheel. In addition, she had to scrunch down to reach the gas and brake pedals. Thank goodness it was an automatic transmission! It was ten miles to my cousin's house. Mom drove very slowly and we arrived safely. Whew! We couldn't stay long, though, because we had to get home before Dad. Mom didn't want him to know she'd taken his precious car for a drive. Rocky and I thought her antics were funny. We made it home again in one piece and with the car intact. To my knowledge, Dad never knew the car had been moved. If he did know, he never said a word to Mom. Those were some of the happiest memories of my childhood.

2. Secrets

Ruth had been born in the United States. Her mother Martina had crossed the Mexican border when she was pregnant with her fourth child. She brought three other children from a previous marriage with her. Family gossip has it that she wanted to give birth here so that this new child would be a U.S. citizen. Martina wanted a better life for her children.

Martina had other children in Mexico who remained with Ruth's father. He didn't want them to go, and he didn't know Martina was pregnant again. Once in the U.S., Martina presumably divorced Ruth's father and married again. Ruth grew up thinking her stepfather was her natural father, and used his last name as hers. She never did have the opportunity to know her siblings or her biological father.

My dad, Joseph, was born and raised in Mexico. Family legend has it that, as a teenager, he and his father rode with Pancho Villa, a well-known bandit and revolutionary in Mexico. His fame stems from being remembered as a hero because he fought for the poor, and for reform for farm and migrant workers. It must have been an exciting adventure for a teenager!

After a few months, Joseph and his father left the group of banditos to care for their own family. Mom told me that when he was in his mid-twenties, he got into a fight with a man who was bullying him. The man got a gun and they struggled. The gun went off, resulting in the man's death. Dad was afraid he might be accused of involuntary manslaughter, since it was uncertain who was holding the gun at the time it went off. Worse yet, he was afraid the man's family or friends might take matters into their own hands and seek revenge through retaliatory actions. His wife at the time helped him escape from Mexico by train to the U.S., hoping that he would be safe there. Dad also knew that his family would be safer if he left the country. He never wanted *us* to visit Mexico because of that incident. I think he was afraid someone would connect us to him and harm us. He never really knew if anyone tried to find him, but he didn't want to risk his life or the safety of either of his beloved families.

Ruth was twenty years old when she met Joseph. He originally told her he was thirty, but in reality he was thirty-eight, eighteen years older than Ruth. He must have really liked Ruth and, wanting to impress her, thought things would go better if she thought he was a younger man. They were married in 1932.

In 1933, at the height of the Depression, Mom became pregnant with Rocky. There was an accident outside the house that startled and frightened Mom so much that she went into early labor and there were complications during childbirth. Rocky was so tiny Mom said he fit into the palm of her hand, and he had to be fed with an eyedropper. He was born with cerebral palsy, which causes his muscles to be spastic, and a few days after his birth, he was stricken with polio. Doctors cautioned Mom and Dad that he may not survive. It seemed to them that the doctors did little to help him. Perhaps their attitude was that since he would not live long it was best to just let nature take its course rather than put such a weak, tiny newborn through what might have turned out to be unnecessary treatments.

The combination of all the medical conditions resulted in stunted growth and limited mobility. When Rocky was five years old, doctors were surprised he had survived that long. They decided to operate on his hips and legs in an effort to uncross them and improve his chances to walk some day on his own. When he was ten years of age, he could walk with leg braces and crutches. At eighteen he could walk somewhat independently, but still with some difficulty. He has always had to wear leg braces.

At times, Rocky's mental abilities were, and still are, those of a young child. Despite all those challenges, amazingly enough, he survived childhood and many years beyond.

When Rocky was just a few weeks old, Mom and Dad were informed that their marriage was invalid because Dad was technically and legally still married to his first wife in Mexico. Prior to that notification, my mother had no idea he was married! What a shock that must have been! Mom's sister, however, was not surprised at the news. She thought he could have been married before because he seemed older than what he said. Ruth did not believe her sister at first. With documented evidence in front of her, however, she had to believe he really was married. She got angry that he had not been up front with her. She still wanted to be with him, though, now more than ever because they had just had Rocky and they were a family. They had to have *their* marriage dissolved, and he had to divorce his first wife in Mexico before he could remarry Ruth. They kept the original marriage license showing they were married in 1932 for Rocky's sake.

On a regular basis, Dad, who could not write, asked Mom to write letters for him to send to his family in Mexico. He had a job working for the Southern Pacific Railroad laying down and repairing tracks, and made a decent wage. In the letters he always included money orders from the post office for his ex-wife and three children.

During WWII, Ruth worked for a manufacturing company that made gaskets for airplane engines and tanks. In the late 1950's, when I was seven or eight years old, I remember Mom going to night school to become an electrician. As she did her homework, she read the questions and answers aloud to me. The new information intrigued me and encouraged me to take an interest in science. Mom never had the opportunity to use her knowledge as an electrician because at that time companies were not hiring women electricians. Instead, she ended up working at a commercial canning factory on the assembly line during canning seasons. I admired her determination to learn a new skill, even if she couldn't use it to get a different job.

Ruth spoke, and could read and write, in both English and Spanish. As a young girl, she won awards in school for accomplishments in her studies, and won contests in handwriting and calligraphy. I thought she had the most beautiful handwriting! She taught me to write as beautifully as she did. She also taught me calligraphy, Spanish, and English. When I was thirteen and fourteen years old, Mom had a job cleaning homes. I went with her during the summer. She used that opportunity to teach me, in great detail, the proper ways to clean and to iron. I remember the homeowners who hired her wanted the top sheets and pillow cases ironed so they would be crisp and fresh. The beds had to be made just so. These people were so particular! One of the two times per week that we were there, we were to be on our hands and knees with a rolled up wet towel, collecting dog hair from the rugs so that the vacuum cleaner would not bog down. Mom was paid fifteen dollars for eight hours of work. At that time, that was good pay!

Ruth and Joseph took good care of Rocky and me. Connie, the woman who had moved next door with her mother, husband, and their four children, also had an effect on my life. I was told the kids whom I played with daily were my cousins. I had little contact with Connie's mother. In fact, I was told I couldn't go visit her because she was very frail and ill. I don't think she was really that ill, but for some reason they didn't want me talking to her. I remember vividly the day she came to our house to visit Ruth and suffered a heart attack. Dad and Mom quickly carried her out to the car to take her to the hospital. I sat in the back seat with her and Mom on the way to the hospital. She died there several hours later. I was only seven years old, but the incident made quite an impression on me. Many years later, I learned that this frail, older woman was in reality my grandmother. I never had the opportunity to meet my other grandparents because they died before I was born, so I am especially sad that I was never able to know the one person I *could* have known as a grandparent.

After my grandmother's death, things changed some at home. With dad having retired from the railroad by this time, our income from his pension and Social Security was less than what he was getting before. Plus, we had mom's stepfather living with us – one more mouth to feed. I was eight years old and such a tomboy I would tear my clothes playing leap frog and jumping fences. Mom had always wanted me to have nice clothes, so she used to replace the ones I tore. After my grandmother's death, and with the change in household income, I was unable to wear new dresses as often. In fact, I remember having to wear my mother's clothes to school. The other kids made fun of my clothes then. They also asked if Mom was my grandmother because she was older than most of the other mothers.

We needed more income to pay bills, so Mom, Dad, Rocky, and I, worked for a local ranch owner picking prunes. We were paid for each ton we picked. Dad's goal was to pick a ton a day; 40 crates to be exact, so that we could pay bills and have money for school clothes and shoes. My dad was frugal, but very generous with his family. At the end of each day on the way home, he would buy us each a 25-cent hamburger and a 10-cent milkshake. That doesn't sound like a lot these days, but back then it was a fair amount compared to the hourly wage.

I didn't know at the time that one of the "bills" my parents had was paying Connie to keep a secret about me. I wonder now if Connie's mother might have been her main source of income, so when she died, Connie needed to find another means of financial support. In her mind, my parents would be that source for her. The other change that seemed to happen was that as I was getting older, Connie felt she should be told everything I was doing. I didn't understand that at all!

Sometimes it seemed that I was expected to take on a lot more responsibility than other children my age. I still vividly remember one incident involving our cats. I brought home a cute little black and white kitten. One of our other cats did not take too well to the new competition and attacked the kitten. In the effort to separate them, Mom's forearm was scratched. It was a deep wound. The doctor prescribed antibiotics and bandaged her arm. We had to change the dressing daily and debride the dying skin. That became my job. It was awful! Due to Mom's diabetes, it took several weeks to heal. That was the beginning of my education in home nursing skills.

After a while, Connie moved from the house next door to us to a different area of East San Jose. She still always wanted to know where I was and what I was doing, and called or came over often. It seemed that Connie wanted to maintain some level of control over me and my parents. She told them that she and her children were put into the will of a very wealthy woman whom she had rescued from the streets. I was told that as long as *I* behaved and didn't get into trouble, once she got the inheritance, she would see that we had a new home. She suggested to Mom and Dad that then Rocky could go to doctors in Switzerland who could fix his legs so he could walk normally. She tried to make me feel that if I didn't do as she said our family would not get any of the inheritance and it would be all *my* fault. I just shrugged it off, thinking, "She's not my mother! She can't tell me what to do!"

I somehow took Connie's promises of inheritance to mean we would be wealthy, and adopted the attitude that I no longer needed to excel at school. I presumed I would never have to work. The things kids misinterpret! I don't know how much truth there was to Connie's story, but, other relatives later confirmed they had heard the same proclamations. No inheritance ever appeared.

As I mentioned previously, it seemed Connie expected Mom and Dad to continue supporting her financially. I remember often walking into the room and seeing Mom hand Connie money. Mom and Dad told me that Connie had a brain tumor and had to go to Los Angeles. She needed the money for airfare, a hotel, and treatments. What I didn't understand was why my mother had to give Connie the money. I was under the impression that Connie's husband had a good job and decent income. Why couldn't he pay for it?

Shortly after Connie moved, the state exercised the right to eminent domain to purchase my parents' home. By this right, the government could take our private property for the purpose of building a freeway in the area as long as they compensated the property owner. They only paid my parents a nominal amount. Like it or not, we had to move. Fortunately, things actually worked out for the better because the new home in North San Jose was in a better location. There were no gangs. There was still a lot of undesirable activity, but there were no dead-end streets or empty fields nearby to worry about.

I was thirteen years old at the time. A lot of my girlfriends from the East side wanted to visit the area. One friend in particular wanted to come over to get away from her mother who, at times, behaved irrationally. One weekend my friend came to stay overnight. She asked Mom if we could go to the movies. Even though it was late, Mom said it was ok. We went to the movies and my girlfriend met some guys there. She left with them, and I stayed in the movie theater until they closed at midnight. I had no place to go after the theater closed, so I went to the pizza parlor next door. I had no money to even call home from a pay phone. Two young men approached me and asked if I needed a ride. They said they would take me home, so I naively said "Okay." Instead of taking me home, they drove to an isolated area by the railroad tracks. By that time, I was frightened and knew I might be in danger. I managed to get out of the car and tried to run, but didn't get far before they caught up with me. They put me back in the car. With two of them and only one of me, I was over-powered. I didn't really understand what they were doing to me – no one had ever discussed sex with me. To put it simply, both of the men took advantage of me. I was now a victim of rape. I knew I had been seriously violated.

When they were done, they started the car and drove me close to home, dropping me off a little ways from my house. Parts of my body were hurting, and I was feeling stunned. I didn't know where I was. I walked and walked until I found a street sign that I recognized. When I arrived home, my girlfriend and her mother were waiting for me. My girlfriend said ***I*** was the one who had taken off. Her mother took the suitcase sitting nearby and started to beat me with it. Dad intercepted and told her to leave me alone, to leave with her daughter and never come back.

I was in a daze and couldn't believe what had happened. I never said a word about the incident to anyone until many years later. I was too embarrassed and afraid. It became my big secret, something that had a significant impact on my life. One immediate effect was that I wore as many clothes as I could:

girdles, garter belts and nylon hosiery, and layers of blouses and sweaters. Mom was a very conservative dresser, and I was not used to wearing skimpy clothes to begin with, especially in public. Now I wanted my body to be even more covered and not accessible to anyone. One time my Godmother brought me a swim suit and made me wear it to the pool at Alum Rock. That was *very* difficult for me. Between what had happened and my usual layers of clothes, I felt so exposed and embarrassed. Naturally, my Godmother didn't know about what had happened, so she didn't understand. She was just trying to help me be a more stylish teenager. As soon as I could, I went back to the comfort of hiding behind layers again.

Shhh … it's a SECRET!!!

Shhh … it's a SECRET!!!

Shhh … it's a SECRET!!!

3. First Love

When I was fourteen years old I met Paul, a nice young man almost five years older than me. We met through one of my girlfriends. He was actually one of the guys *she* was dating. I wasn't looking for anyone. Whenever I looked at myself in the mirror, I didn't think I was pretty enough. I'd been told so many times by some family members that they didn't think I was pretty at all. I believed them. At the time, I actually liked my girlfriend's brother, but I was too shy to say anything.

Paul told me it was love at first sight for him. After he met me, he broke up with my girlfriend and then asked her for my phone number and address. She actually liked another guy, so she wasn't upset when they stopped dating or that he was asking for my phone number. She called me right away to tell me that he was going to ask me out. I told her I liked him, too, and thought he was cute.

When Paul came to my house the first time, he asked my parents if he could take me to the movies. They said yes. We didn't go to the movies, though. Instead, we walked and talked. He told me all about himself, that he had played football, been in the high school ROTC program, and played the saxophone. After graduation he went to work as an auto detailer for car dealerships and private parties. We walked for hours on end that day. My feet were so tired I couldn't walk anymore! He called my parents to let them know we wanted to stop at the neighborhood soda shop and creamery for a bite to eat. The respect he showed my parents by communicating with them earned a lot of points with Mom and Dad! It was a "dreamy" first date.

We wanted to spend time together and continued to see each other as often as we could. He had no car, so usually took the bus home. My parents trusted him so much that one evening when it was raining hard, they told him he could stay overnight. They didn't want him to risk getting sick from being out in the cold and rain.

When I was in the ninth grade, my parents planned a birthday party for me at our house. They moved the dining room table out of the dining room to make that the dance area. My friend Leo, a singer in a local high school band, offered to play at the party. Of course, I said, "Sure!" The highlight of the party was when Leo sang *Earth Angel* to me. I was in heaven. What was funny was that I didn't know a lot of the people there because I only invited a few friends. When word got out that there was a party, everyone in the junior high school wanted to come. The police knew there was a party and stopped by to make sure everything was going okay. They asked if my parents were home, which they were, and if there was alcohol being served. At fifteen, there definitely was no alcohol served in *my* house! The band had black lights and flashing strobe lights to add to the party atmosphere. The house lights were turned down, and many of the kids were making out in various places. Paul and I stayed on the dance floor. How could we do anything else with my parents in the house?

After a few weeks, Paul told his parents that he wanted to marry me. His parents thought he was a mature adult. Being the second to the youngest in the family of ten children he had become very responsible, and would be capable of taking care of a family. They gave their blessings to let us marry.

Respecting the traditions of the Hispanic culture, Paul and his parents came to my house to ask Ruth and Joseph for my hand in holy matrimony. Dad, being from Mexico where one married young, said yes right away. Mom wasn't too sure. I think part of it was that she worried about what would happen to Rocky if I married. Would I continue to take care of him? And would Paul's family accept Rocky?

Connie happened to be at the house when Paul and his parents arrived, so she heard the proposal. She always seemed to think she could control my life. Somehow, she managed to persuade both of my parents *not* to give their blessings. I believe she had other plans for me and thought it best to cut Paul out of my life completely. What she didn't realize was that Paul was determined that we were going to be together.

I wanted to be honest with Paul, and felt I should tell him about the attack that had happened near the railroad tracks. I told him if he no longer wanted to get married after hearing that, I would understand. He hugged me and said, "It's not your fault. How could I blame you for something you had no control over? I still want to marry you. I love you."

Two weeks later, Paul and his parents came to my house for a second time, again asking my parents for my hand in marriage. Dad asked me if I loved Paul, and I told him, "I do." He looked at Mom, who didn't get a chance to say anything. Again, Connie was there, interfering, telling my parents not to let us get married. She asked, "What does a fourteen-year-old know about love?" I think she was really thinking, what would *she* do if she lost control over me. Connie was persistent and Mom and Dad again said no.

Disappointed, Paul and I left the house and went onto the front porch. He asked me if I really wanted to marry him. I told him, "I love you, and, yes, I want to marry you." He thought if we had a baby, my parents would *not* listen to Connie, and would finally agree to bless our marriage. Even though I had *no* idea what it meant to make a baby, I said yes. I had been told by my parents that storks bring babies and deliver them through the chimney! As a child, I had asked Mom and Dad to build a fireplace and chimney so we could have more kids. Boy! Was I surprised when I found out what it *really* took to make a baby!

I got pregnant right away, but, I was so inexperienced, and no one had explained such things to me, so I didn't realize it. By the time I was five months along, I started eating a lot more. Connie noticed, and talked my Mom into taking me to the doctor. She went with us to the appointment, and the doctor confirmed that I was pregnant. Connie asked how far along, thinking she could get me to have an abortion. Fortunately, it was too late to consider that as an option. Connie was *not* happy.

Dad, on the other hand, was happy for us. He would take me to the drug store where there was a great snack counter and buy me whatever I wanted to eat. Mom was resigned to the idea. I think she realized that I was the only person who could give her grandchildren, so in some ways she may have also been happy for us. Connie, however, was determined to do something about it to keep us from getting married. She went to the police and accused Paul of statutory rape because I was a minor and Paul was over eighteen. He was put in jail. She also told the police that I was not in my right mind and not capable of making decisions. In the late 60's just about anything could be said and you could be put in jail. Individual rights were few and far between. They even put me in juvenile hall! After a few hours, just enough time to scare me, I was released into my parents' custody. Because I was pregnant, I was not allowed to go back to public school, so an independent study teacher came to the house to work with me on my tenth grade requirements. Connie told my parents not to let me out of their sight because she knew I would try to see Paul.

At that time, it seemed to me that parents could make all

the decisions concerning their daughter's care, and that of her unborn child. I had no rights. With me being a minor, and Connie trying to control my parents as well, she tried to persuade them to put the baby up for adoption right after birth. Dad was really upset. He and Mom were afraid of losing their grandchild to a stranger, but Connie was very persistent. The court did not require permission from the baby's father for an adoption, and Paul was unable to protest because he was in jail. My baby was going to be adopted, whether I agreed to it or not. I was devastated.

Connie thought that with Paul in jail, our forced separation would destroy my relationship with him, but it actually strengthened our bond. He wrote me letters every day, and would tell me how much he loved me. Sometimes he wrote loving poems and drew art work to send to me. I promised him I'd wait, and that we'd one day be together.

4. Mother, Wife and more...

When it was time for our baby to be born, my parents and Connie went with me to the hospital. Paul was still in jail, so he wasn't able to be there. They anesthetized me so I wouldn't be awake during the delivery, and when I came to, my baby girl had been taken from me. The day after she was born, they brought her in so I could see her. I named her Linda. I knew she was going to be adopted, and I didn't know what to feel. It was all very difficult for me. Paul was in jail so I couldn't be with him, and I wasn't at all confident that I knew how to be a mother. Because the baby had been taken away from me right after her birth, I didn't feel the bonding attachment I imagined new mothers usually feel. It was overwhelming.

There was a medical problem as well. The doctors explained to my mother and me that Linda should have been a twin, but the other fetus did not develop fully. Somehow some of the organs from both fetuses merged into one body. Consequently, Linda was born with double the normal number of kidneys and ureters. The ureters were tightly intertwined in her tiny body and connected to one bladder. They could not operate to remove the extra organs because the extra kidneys, connecting tubes, and veins could not be separated from each other without endangering her life. This put a lot of stress on most of her internal bodily functions. She was very weak and needed to stay in the hospital for a few days after I was released. When she was strong enough, my parents and I took her home. As her body developed over the years, we found she also had two sets of teeth, and other signs that there had been another fetus that had not developed. I wasn't sure how to care for any baby, so the extra challenges we might face with Linda worried me even more.

I guess that any charges against Paul were dropped because within a few days of Linda's birth, he was released from jail. He and his parents came for a third time to ask for my hand in marriage. Connie was there again. Dad was not home at the time and she convinced my mother *again* to deny the marriage, despite the fact we now were parents of a beautiful little girl. Paul left with his parents, planning to return soon with diapers. After they left, Connie told me that my parents had tried to adopt Linda, but the judge would not allow it because they were too old. They were allowed, however, to be her legal guardians. She further stated that I would not be allowed to have any say in her care, medical needs, or upbringing. Things felt so out of my control! It didn't seem right! I was frightened, hurt, and angry. I was admittedly nervous about how to care for her, but I didn't want anyone else to have Linda. Our bond had started to form. She was *my* baby. I loved her and wanted to care for her myself. Very quietly and discreetly I started to pack things she needed in a bag. I made sure to pack enough milk, diapers, blankets, and clothes.

When Paul returned with the diapers, I told him what Connie had said, and we both agreed we had to take Linda and leave. He called his sister to let her know we would be at his grandfather's house. She heard later that we were reported to the police as runaways. I was worried that because Paul was older, he would be put in jail again. I called Mom, telling her I thought what Connie was doing was wrong. I asked her, "How would you feel if it was you and someone was taking your baby away? We want to be married and be a family, just like you, Dad, Rocky and me. I don't want to come home if Connie is going to cause more problems and try to put Paul back in jail. He has been very respectful to you and Dad. He takes good care of Linda and me.

Paul doesn't deserve to be treated that way. Please, think about that."

After a couple of days, Mom consented to our marriage. Dad said, "We'll agree to this marriage, but you have to live with us in our house." He explained that Paul needed to understand that once they were no longer able to care for Rocky, I would have that responsibility. In addition, as they were older parents, they might need care themselves someday.

We left Paul's grandfather's home and moved in with Mom and Dad. Connie told them not to show me the guardianship papers in case I might try to contest the judge's decision. I assumed that since they were finally consenting to our marriage, they would no longer maintain guardianship of Linda and that Paul and I could be totally responsible for her well-being.

Paul and I were soon married in a civil ceremony. It wasn't the type of wedding I had always dreamt about. I wanted to wear a white wedding dress with a beautiful flowing veil, and have Dad walk me down the aisle. "I promise you, Anita," Paul said, "I'll give you the wedding you want some day."

Life as a newlywed was great. We were married and enjoying life with our little girl. Nothing is ever perfect or without challenges, however. One of my front teeth had decayed and been filled when I was ten years old. The dentist told me then that I didn't have enough calcium in my system, and that my teeth were weak. The filling had to be replaced a few years later when, as a crossing guard at school, I bumped that tooth. Shortly after our wedding, that filling fell out, leaving an embarrassing, gaping hole. A few days later, I became very ill and was in pain. Paul and Dad took me to the dentist, who found I had an abscess. He prescribed antibiotics and told me to come back when the swelling went down so that he could pull the tooth and make a bridge. When I went for that appointment, the dentist put me under anesthesia to pull the tooth. I was only sixteen years old, so I didn't question being put under for pulling just one tooth, and I trusted the dentist. When I woke up, I found he had pulled sixteen top teeth, and *all* the lower back molars! He told me they were all going to go bad eventually, so he thought he would save me some misery by pulling them in advance. I was shocked, somewhat panicked, and thought, 'What did he do to me?'

I had to go for three months with no teeth because the swelling needed to subside before they could make the molds for dentures and partial plates. It was so hard to eat! And I never smiled. It was a tough three months. Finally the molds were taken, I got new teeth and I was able to eat and smile again. I was a happy camper!

At the end of that summer, Paul, Linda, and I moved from my parents' home into a three-room cottage, still in San Jose, but out in the boonies on a horse ranch. It was small with only about 250 square feet, but it would have to do. Paul was working for his friend at the auto detailing garage, but income was very limited. Financially, the cottage was a bargain at $75 per month, utilities included. However, there were five-inch red bugs, huge rats, and aggressive animals who tried to enter the house. During this time, one of Paul's sisters and her husband came to live with us in this tiny little cottage. It was very cramped, especially when other family members stopped by on a daily basis. We had no time to ourselves. I was pregnant with our second child and emotions were running high. The landlord was not pleased that more people were living there than they allowed, so that Fall he told us we needed to leave.

I didn't want to return to my parents' house and impose on them. Paul and I wanted to be responsible in our decisions and cope on our own with any situations that might come up. One of Paul's other sisters lived in a little residential area on top of Little Uvas Road, near Uvas County Park in the Santa Cruz Mountains. Just past her house, we found a vacant cabin in the woods. The cabin was not equipped with a bathroom, but there was at least an outhouse. The only running water in the house came through the pipe from the creek. There was no electricity, but there was a wood-burning stove where we could boil our water before drinking it, and where we cooked food. The only other source of heat was a huge fireplace built with river rock. The three of us were able to sleep cozily in the small day bed.

As the weeks passed, the rainy season started and the temperatures got colder. To get to the cabin, we had to cross a bridge. The truck tires had to be positioned just right on the bridge to roll over it. One evening when we were coming home, the bridge was slippery, and the truck tires started to slide. Paul tried to correct the tires, but then the truck slid in the other direction. Finally, the front tires of the truck caught on a tree. We were hanging over the ravine, dangling, and worried the truck would fall into the rushing creek below, with us in it! It was a very scary situation. Not only was I afraid of the fall, but the creek had a significant amount of water, and I had an intense fear of drowning. A few years before, I almost drowned in a swimming pool. Several kids had been teasing me about not knowing how to swim. Once in the water, they pulled me under the surface. I panicked, and my arms were flailing. They thought I was trying to hit them, so they pulled me down further. When I was finally able to get to the top again, I grabbed the edge of the pool and got out. I fell to the ground, gasping and coughing up water. Then they knew I was not just joking with them. I really did have a serious fear of being in the water.

Paul managed to carefully climb out of the truck, hoping to redistribute the weight so the truck would tip forward more than backward. That worked and he was able to climb out and go to his sister's to get help. Unfortunately, no one was home. He came back to get Linda and me out of the truck, hoping to do so without the truck falling into the ravine. He finally got us out. Scared and shaken, we walked to the cabin. Paul went back to the truck, trying to think of a way to get it back on solid ground again. When his sister and her husband came home, they used their vehicle to pull the truck, and all was well again. After that experience, I could never go over a bridge without feeling anxious. For a long time, I never went *anywhere* that required driving over a bridge. I was so happy when my parents asked us to move back in with them!

We moved back into their house in November, when I was seven months pregnant, and we enjoyed Thanksgiving and Christmas with my parents and Rocky. In January, the day I went into labor, Mom was home, but there was no one there with a car to take me, so I walked three and a half blocks to the hospital. I walked into the emergency room and they asked me what was wrong. They quickly found out when during a sharp labor pain, I shouted, "I'm having a baby!!!" They rushed me to the labor room. From there, they barely had time to get me into the delivery room before our second daughter arrived. It was all of thirty minutes from the time I arrived at the hospital until I gave birth. I was admitted to the hospital, spent one night, and, contrary to the typical three-day stays, I signed us out the next day. I wanted to be home with my beautiful new baby girl and the rest of my family.

Several months later, one of Paul's sisters asked us to move in with her family to help pay the rent. We were only there one month and they asked us to leave because Paul had lost his detailing job and we no longer had any income. We wanted to make sure our daughters were well cared for, so we asked my parents to take care of them for us until Paul got another job and we were financially on our feet again. Paul and I didn't want to add further to our parents' living expenses, so we lived in our car for the next month. We found work wherever we could. We lived off candy bars and cheap food, giving every spare dime we had to Mom to help pay for supplies for the girls. We were determined to demonstrate that we were fit parents.

When Paul got an offer for paid training in the art of dry walling and carpentry, we moved back in with my parents He was very supportive of what I wanted to do, too. He knew that I loved to style hair, and that I wanted to be financially independent. When we had enough income to support our family, he encouraged me by paying my tuition so I could attend a local beauty school. I had finished eleventh grade, but not graduated high school. The beauty school needed proof that I had completed at least tenth grade. While looking for the paper I needed in my parents' files, I found the legal document granting them guardianship for Linda. I was very upset that they had completed that paperwork and had not filed new documents to relinquish guardianship of Linda when Paul and I got married. What bothered me more was that they had kept it a secret from me all this time. When I confronted my mother, she said she had forgotten all about the guardianship because by now we had been married for two years and she was convinced that we were capable of being responsible parents. She hadn't thought about the old paperwork in months.

The next day Paul and I went to the county offices and filed a petition to regain custody of Linda. We proved to the county that we were employed by virtue of the job training and attending beauty school. The judge accepted our petition that day. Linda was legally ours again!

Life was going well. We were a family and both employed. Paul enjoyed spoiling me with beautiful dresses, the children had nice clothes, and we had good food. Paul had been assigned a job doing drywall, helping build a new structure for the Boys Club of America in the Saratoga/Los Gatos area. His name was inscribed with the other construction workers on one of the plaques on display in the building. We were both very proud of his participation in that project.

During our court appearance to regain custody of Linda, the judge assigned a county social worker to help us with housing. The social worker knew I was helping to care for my parents, and helped us obtain housing in a duplex near their home.

Soon after that move, Paul kept his promise to give me the wedding I dreamed about. On Valentine's Day, 1970, we exchanged our vows and renewed our commitment to each other in the church. Both of our families were present. I asked a girlfriend to be my bridesmaid, and our little Linda was the flower girl. Just as I had always hoped, Dad walked me down the aisle. I wore a white dress with a flowing veil. My dream was coming true! We had a reception at my parents' house after the wedding. It was a beautiful day! I felt our marriage now meant so much more, being tied together with the lasso that had been blessed by the priest.

At the time of our church wedding, I was unknowingly three months pregnant with our third child, a son. Our children would have each other to be with, to love, to fight with, to say I am sorry to. I didn't want them to be alone like I'd been growing up. Each of my children was a welcomed blessing. They were at times challenging. I certainly learned a lot from them and the experience of being a parent. I loved being a Mom and was happy our family was expanding.

5. Heartbreak

In April, less than three months after our church wedding, Paul became seriously ill. It seemed that almost overnight he had no energy, and he didn't look like himself. He walked around as if he were continually in and out of sleep. He told me, "Something's wrong. I just don't feel right." We called the advice nurse at the hospital, and after asking him a few questions, some of which he couldn't answer, I talked to her. She told me that I should take him to the Emergency Room as soon as possible. At this point, I didn't realize how truly sick he was.

Before leaving for the hospital, Paul sat on our bed and asked me to bring him the girls. Linda was two and half years old. I brought her to him first. He didn't have the strength to pick her up, so I placed her on the bed. He looked at her and told her, "Be a good girl. I love you." Then I took our other daughter to see him. She was only fifteen months old. He kissed her, lovingly patted her little bottom, and told me to put her back into her crib. Then he looked at me and said, "I'm ready to go." I didn't know this would be the last time he would see his daughters.

A family member who was living with us at the time stayed with the girls. Paul was so weak that I needed help getting him into the car. Fortunately, Paul's brother was visiting that day and could help me. On the way to the hospital, Paul passed out and we couldn't wake him up. When we arrived, the emergency room staff was waiting for us and took him inside.

Once in an exam room, the nurse began asking me a lot of questions. I didn't have answers for most of them. Until that day, Paul hadn't let on to me on that he wasn't feeling well. I had noticed that lately when he came home he would lie down for an hour or so. I just thought he was tired after the long work day.

After the doctor examined Paul, he told me that Paul had severe diabetes. Mom and my brother both struggled with it, but I had no idea that Paul had it, too! The doctor, concerned with saving Paul's life, told me very bluntly, "If we don't give your husband 1,000 ccs of insulin immediately, he'll be dead by morning." The news hit me like a ton of bricks. I couldn't understand how one minute my seemingly healthy, twenty-three-year-old husband could now be on the verge of death. They gave him the insulin and immediately moved him from the ER to the Intensive Care Unit. I was only allowed to stay with him there for a few minutes at a time.

I was five months pregnant. With all that was going on, I started to feel sick. The medical staff thought that I might be going into pre-mature labor. I insisted they call my obstetrician. He came to the ER to see me, and determined that I was not going into labor, but I was *very* stressed. He sat with me, tried to calm me down, and had the nurse give me something mild to help me relax. He was very upset with the hospital staff for having been so inconsiderate in the blunt way they had told me that Paul might die within a few hours without treatment. My doctor felt they could have been tactfully honest without being so sharply blunt.

He cautioned me, "You have to calm down for your baby. It's not good for either of you." He reassured me that they would keep me updated about Paul's condition.

Paul woke up and asked for me. He made me promise that I would not leave him. Under the circumstances, the hospital allowed me to stay with him, and I stayed at his bedside all night. He was connected to a heart monitor, oxygen, and an IV. Even with the high dose of insulin, he was slipping away. One of the few things Paul told me that night was that our new baby was a boy. I will never know how he knew that, but he did. I trusted him, and we discussed baby names for boys. He wanted me to go against the tradition of naming a son after his father. Instead, he wanted his son to be named Miguel.

In the morning, my mother-in-law arrived. She was upset that I was there, partly because she had been told that she could *not* stay full time with him. ICU rules restrict visitors to only one family member in the room, and usually for only ten minutes at a time. It was because Paul's condition was so serious that the staff bent the rule and allowed me to stay in his room all the time. I was his wife, Paul wanted me there, and after the obstetrician's reprimand they were trying to keep me calm.

Paul's mother walked past the nurse's station and right into his room. She started to yell at me. "How did he get so sick? It's your fault that he's like this! Do you have someone else? I know you do! That white baby of yours isn't my son's! It can't be! You wanted this to happen! You want him to die!" It was embarrassing to hear her shouting such false accusations where anyone could hear them. Linda and our second daughter had different complexions, eye, and hair color. In those days, not many people in the layman's world knew much about genes, DNA, and inherited features, so his mother was convinced that the girls had to have different fathers. In her mind, that could be the *only* reason they could look so different. The truth was that Paul and I had different color traits. One daughter had inherited my color genes, the other Paul's. Since Paul and I were married, she was accusing me of going outside our marriage vows and having an affair. It was very difficult for me being so falsely accused.

Upon hearing the loud commotion, the nurse assigned to Paul's care entered the room. She told us she could hear us all the way down the hall and to "Shut up!" She told my mother-in-law to calm down. Paul's mother then told me that as she was his mother she would stay with him and that I should leave. I explained to her that I had promised Paul I would be there for him, that I wouldn't leave his side. The argument went back and forth until, exhausted and angry, we *both* decided to leave, a decision I would later regret.

I reluctantly went home, exhausted and worried. Paul's mother stayed with me at the house, probably to make sure that if she couldn't be with him, then neither could I. At home I ate a little and checked on my mother. She was very sick, too. With Paul's diagnosis of diabetes and being so close to death, it brought home the fact that Mom and my brother's diabetes could take them from me some day also.

Shortly after checking on Mom, I received a phone call that Paul was conscious again and asking for me. His liver and kidneys were shutting down quickly, though. Before we could get back to the hospital, he had a massive heart attack and died. It was frustrating that the medical staff refused to let us view his body or say good-bye to him. I wonder if that was due to the loud argument his mother and I had the night before. They didn't want to see or hear another confrontation that would likely disturb other patients.

My mother-in-law had called other members of their family the night before, telling them to go see Paul. They gathered at the hospital that morning. I had to be the bearer of the sad news that it was too late. He had died. They were really upset. In their eyes, I was to blame for his death. They thought that I should have noticed that he was ill. Even the two family members who had been living with us accused me of killing him. They all wanted to believe it was entirely my fault that he died. I was devastated enough at losing my husband. I didn't need to hear things like that. It seemed that his family was not considering what **I** might be feeling and going through. I was eighteen, the mother of two daughters, and five months pregnant with another baby. The man I loved and thought I would spend the rest of my life with had just died. Paul and our children were the center of my world. When he died, my world crumbled. I guess they were so wrapped up in their own shock and grief, looking for someone or something to blame that they were ignoring the effects it was having on me and how it would affect our children. It was clear they would not support me emotionally or help us in the future.

While growing up I was exposed to different religions and other forms of spirituality. I dabbled in astrology and numerology, and had contact with people who had psychic abilities. As a young adult I continued to have a spiritual connection with God, and developed the belief that events happen for a reason. I came to believe that even the family you are born into is pre-destined. We have to deal with these events, good or bad, in the right manner. Whatever manner that is, it is up to us to decide the best way for each of us to deal with events and situations in our lives. That is what I did. I dealt with Paul's family as best I could, and proceeded to make arrangements for his funeral. With my mother's help, we arranged a traditional Catholic service.

Paul's family asked me *not* to bring the girls to the service, but I decided to let Linda come with me. She was a sensitive and smart child, and had not seen him since the day he left for the hospital. I felt it was important that she understand that her father did not leave her by his choice. I explained to her as best I could that her father was very sick and had died. He went to heaven. During the service she tugged at my shirt and asked, "Mommy, is my Daddy in that box over there?"

I collected my thoughts and said, "Yes, his body is in that box, but his spirit is with God." She seemed to accept my simple answer. Over the next few months, it seemed she accepted that he was gone, at least as much as a three-year-old could. She would tell me, "Daddy's okay." It was so sweet of her to reassure me. It helped seeing that she seemed to be doing okay.

Three days after the funeral, I felt a connection with Paul. He appeared in a dream that night, and many other nights over the next couple of months. It was always the same dream. I would see a wall with a window. Paul was on the other side of the window and would lift me up and bring me over to his side. On that side was another world filled with brilliant color. There was a beautiful oak tree, green grass, and colorful flowers. He always had a picnic prepared for us. We would talk and spend time together. It was wonderful. After a while, he would say "It's time to go home now." He would take me back to the wall, and once I climbed back through the window, I would wake up. When I awoke, I could never recall everything we said, but I always felt as if I'd been with him and that he was comforting me. These dreams helped me cope with the reality that he was gone, and eased my pain. I believed I would see him again when I die, but the dreams made living without him now more bearable.

6. Life after Paul - Fight or Flight?

My relationship with Paul's family was distant after his death. They did come to the house once to see Miguel. My suspicion is that they mostly wanted to see if he bore any resemblance to Paul. Miguel has the lighter skin coloring from my side of the family. His eyes and hair color are just like Paul's. Once they left, I didn't see them again for many years.

Paul's brother Vincent wanted me to marry him. According to his interpretation of the *Bible*, a brother should take responsibility for the widow of his deceased brother by marrying her. I turned down his offer. I was not in love with him, and after the way the family had thrown such horrible accusations at me, I wanted to keep my distance from them. I couldn't be certain they would not turn on me again.

My parents encouraged me to move out of the duplex where Paul and I had lived. They always said they wanted me to live with them, and they could use my help caring for Rocky. Raising three small children at nineteen would have been difficult doing it on my own. It seemed the move would help all of us, so the kids and I moved in with Mom and Dad.

My father gave me a car so I could take the kids to appointments, run errands, and look for a job. During one of my trips to the pediatrician, I was getting ready to turn left onto a bridge. After our experience with the bridge in Uvas County Park, I was already nervous about going over it, but that was the only route I could take. Another car was approaching from the left. As I started to make my turn, the other car sped up. It felt like the car was aiming for me! In an effort to move out of the way, I swerved and hit the side wall of the bridge. The speeding car never stopped, just drove off.

The girls were with me in the car. Passenger cars didn't have seat belts or car seats for children back then. The girls fell off their seats and onto the floor. Both were scared and crying, but, thankfully, they were not hurt. As I was calming them down, a police car arrived. He asked for my license and the car registration. When he found out that the car belonged to my father, he said, "I'm not going to give you a ticket because I know you're going to have a hard enough time explaining this to your father!" I was thankful he was so kind and didn't give me a ticket.

As I drove home, I thought about how I would explain the incident to Dad. When I drove into the driveway, seeing the damaged front fender and broken headlight, Dad asked what had happened. When I told him about the accident, he was more concerned with finding out if *we* were okay than about the condition of the car. He said he could always replace the car, but he couldn't replace us. Dad loved us so much!

After living in the neighborhood for a few months, new people moved in next door to us. I met the woman first. Her name was Lena, and she was living with her boyfriend Art. Art's nephew, Dick, spent a lot of time there, too. He talked to us in the front yard almost every day. We passed each other on the street when I took my children to the store or the park. He was a few years older than me, and in the Army. He seemed to be interested in me, but, the attraction was not mutual. After a few weeks, he asked my parents if he could take me out. My parents were impressed with him, so they gave their permission. I wasn't ready for another relationship, and I had to think about my children and how they would respond to a new man in their life. I wasn't sure I wanted to go out with *anyone* just yet.

Lena suggested that she, Art, Dick, and I go out on a double date to make it more comfortable for me. We went to a bar where there was music and dancing. Much to my surprise, I had a good time. I still felt Dick was not my type, but it was a new experience for me to date without being in a committed relationship. I discovered it was fun!

My parents didn't mind babysitting while I was out, but Connie made no qualms about saying how she felt. In essence, she told me I was being a bad mother, and that I shouldn't ask my mother to babysit. She thought I should be getting my life in order and looking for a husband to take care of us so we would not be a burden on my parents. She may have been thinking about my parents, but it felt more like her typical efforts to control my life. I was over eighteen now, a mother, and trying to be independent. I didn't want her advice or suggestions. I ignored her comments. I also knew that Mom enjoyed spending time with the kids, teaching the girls how to sew on buttons and bake cookies. She wanted me to be happy and enjoy life. Mom really didn't mind babysitting her grandchildren while I went out.

One day when I was out with another male friend and some of my girlfriends, they got the idea we should go to Reno for the day. I had no clue how far Reno was from San Jose, and assumed it was nearby, so I didn't tell Mom and Dad where I was going or how long I would be gone. When I came back that night, Mom, Connie, and Dad were waiting for me. They had been worried because they didn't know where I was. Keep in mind we didn't have cell phones then to make phone calls convenient, if I'd even thought to call them. They obviously couldn't get in touch with me either. Connie began yelling and screaming at me. She said I had been irresponsible, that I needed to change my ways or she would step in and take my children from me. I became defensive. I told Connie that she wasn't my mother, and to butt out. She hadn't been there to help with the family before when I could have used some help. There was no way she was going to get between me and my children now!

Connie made such a fuss that Dick heard the commotion and came over to add his two cents. For some reason he was under the impression I was exclusively *his* girlfriend, and didn't like me running off with another man even for a day. He was afraid he would lose me, not realizing he didn't *have* me to begin with! His way of fixing the situation was to ask me to marry him. I replied, "Really? I don't love you! Why would you want to marry someone who doesn't love you?"

"Just marry me, just marry me!" he insisted.

I told him, "You have nothing to offer me. You have no money, no car, and you are living in one room in someone else's house. There isn't enough room for us and my three children there. I have too many responsibilities to take on another one. What do you take me for? I won't marry you!"

I thought hearing these things would discourage him. To shut him up, I naively told him, "If you can get the money to get us married in Reno and come back, I guess I'll marry you." I really thought he wouldn't be able to do it.

I'd just been approved through Section Eight housing to rent a three-bedroom, furnished apartment for just pennies on the dollar. I hoped Mom wouldn't tell Dick about that. Unfortunately, she was so happy for me at the prospect of another marriage that she told Dick about the apartment. In a few days he came back with a car and money, saying, "I got everything you asked for. You have the new apartment for us to live in. Now you have to marry me! You said if I got these things, you would."

Dad always taught me that a person's word is their integrity. If you gave your word, you had to keep it. Since I had said I would marry Dick if he got a car and money to support us, I felt obligated now to marry him. I told him again, "You know I don't love you. I'm just doing this because I gave you my word, and I will keep it." I shouldn't have lived up to my word this time, but it seemed the right thing to do at the moment.

We drove to Reno and were married in one of those tacky little chapels where you pay for your license and quickly exchange vows. I wore a black miniskirt and white go-go boots. My hair was done up in a big beehive hairdo. It sure wasn't the wedding of *my* dreams!

After the ceremony, we drove back to San Jose, picked the kids up from my parents, and went to the new apartment. The Social Services agency was also helping me by giving me a grant of several hundred dollars to pay for things like utilities and other household expenses. On top of that, I was receiving almost two thousand dollars in Survivor Death Benefits from Paul's Social Security benefits. My father had given me a car, and I didn't carry any debt. Dick knew about the Survivor benefits, but not the grant money. It occurred to me much later that my financial backing was probably the key reason he wanted to marry me.

I was so tired after the long day, I just wanted to get the kids to bed and relax. But, Dick said he wanted to talk to me about a few things, so I told him we could talk after the kids were asleep. Once things had calmed down, I went to the living room and asked Dick what he wanted to talk about. He said, "I know you don't love me, but that doesn't matter. Now you belong to me. You have to do whatever I want."

I responded, "As long as you know that my kids *always* come first. You and no one else will ever be first."

He argued with me that as my husband he should be Number One. I think many men may feel this way, but it seems more prevalent within certain cultures, one of them being the traditional Mexican culture. I told him that I meant what I said about the kids coming first. He got up and attacked me, yelling verbal obscenities. The neighbors heard me screaming and started pounding on the wall, so he left the apartment. He left me with bruises and two black eyes. The commotion woke the kids up and they called out to me, asking "What's the matter?"

I didn't want to alarm the kids, so I just said I fell down and "Mommy's okay."

Dick returned the next day and apologized. That was the beginning of a vicious cycle of beatings and apologies. Dick would say, "I'm sorry. I was out of control. It won't happen again." But it did happen, again and again. He never changed. When I went shopping I wore sunglasses to hide my black eyes. It helped me cope to focus on the kids. No matter what was happening in my life, no matter how bad it was, I would do everything within my power to provide for and protect them.

Things would be fine for a couple of days, and then the beatings would start again. This continued for months. I became even more passive about our relationship. I didn't care about him, and I definitely regretted marrying him.

One day while Dick went to Lena's house to visit his uncle, I went next door to spend time with Mom and Dad. In the evening, I went to tell Dick it was time to go home. I was used to visiting Lena, and she always told me to just knock and come in, so I knocked and went in as usual, calling out, "Dick!" He was on the couch having sex with another woman. She was older, had dyed blonde hair, and her body looked large. She looked at me, told me she was a prostitute, and proceeded to get mad at *me* for interrupting them! She stood up. Pulling out a switchblade, she yelled, "You can't hold your man, so he came looking for me."

I wasn't angry. I felt nothing but disgust and stared coldly at her. "If you want him, you can have him. I never fight over a piece of meat. Garbage goes with garbage. But, I'm not willing to take the garbage out. I think the garbage can sit and rot for a while. To be honest, you've taken a big burden off me."

I told Dick, "You know I don't love you. Why would you even think this would bother me? Why do you want to stay married to me? You can leave if you want. I don't care. I guess you must have paid for her services in advance because she just walked out the door." When we got home, Dick was so angry that I had told him off in front of his prostitute that he started beating me.

Dick turned out to be quite the Casanova. Another time I found him at Lena's again with a different woman. This time it was Lois, a woman whom I *thought* was my best friend. Since I didn't love him, it didn't bother me that he was with another woman. He could do what he wanted with whomever he wanted. It *did* bother me that it was with my best friend. To my way of thinking, friends do not treat each other like that. If she wanted him that badly, all she had to do was ask. As far as I was concerned, she could have him!!

After that incident, I told Dick I wanted a divorce. He said he would never give me a divorce. I told myself I didn't have to stay with him. I wanted to leave. I could have moved back in with my parents, but I was too embarrassed. They didn't know about the abuse. All I knew for sure was that this couldn't continue. I needed a plan, and, at this point, I didn't have one.

The next day, I decided to talk to Lena about Dick. The front door was open. I walked in, calling out as I usually did to let her know I was coming in. I went into her bedroom looking for her and found her lying motionless on the bed. Her eyes were open, and her skin was very pale. I touched her, and she was warm. I thought she had passed out. I went to the phone and called Dick at work, asking him to help me take her to the hospital four blocks away. We carried her to the car. When we got to the hospital, I ran inside to get someone to take her into the emergency room. They brought a gurney and got her out of the car. As she was being wheeled into the building, I heard them say she was DOA (Dead on Arrival). Because she was dead before getting to the hospital, the police needed to investigate and asked me a lot of questions. I told them how I had found her and answered what questions I could. I never heard anything more about it after that day.

Lena's boyfriend Art arranged the funeral services. She was young, only twenty-eight years old. She had no family in the area except for her young son. It was a very simple service. Her body was in a closed casket, then taken by the Neptune Society for cremation and scattering her ashes at sea. No one ever spoke about the cause of her death. Paul was the only other young person I knew who had died. This was an experience I never got over. I never enter anyone's house anymore without being greeted at the door, even if the owner tells me to just walk in. I don't want any more surprises like that one!

Life does go on for survivors. Dick, the kids, and I went back to our upstairs apartment. A few days later, complaints were made to the apartment manager about all the noise coming from our unit. We were told to move immediately to a downstairs apartment. We were lucky one was available. One night, Dick became very drunk and beat me mercilessly. Miguel was crying, so I went to his crib in our bedroom to comfort him and moved him to the playpen in the girls' room. I climbed into the playpen with him and curled up into a ball. I felt it was a safe place. Oddly enough, Dick didn't come after me. Looking back now, I remember that he had been in the Vietnam War. His family had told me he sometimes talked about young children in Vietnam being used to carry explosives to blow up areas where soldiers were stationed. I think perhaps Dick's experiences there lead to a post-traumatic stress condition, and that is why he left me alone when I curled up with Miguel.

The next morning, I got up to feed the kids. It was just before Christmas, and Dick started arguing with me in front of them. It didn't matter what we fought about. Dick would pick a fight just to fight, or to try to get me to do what he wanted. It seemed to be purely a control issue. Maybe it was part of his ego and macho self-image that he had to be in control over 'his woman'. This particular day the fight escalated more than usual, and he angrily threw one of my kids roughly into the pantry. I lost it. He had hurt my child. No one gets away with hurting my children!

I grabbed a cast iron skillet and blindly struck him repeatedly. I was so angry I didn't care or even notice where I hit him. I just needed to fight back. When I had stunned him enough, I got all of the children into the bedroom. I told them, "Stay here. Mommy will be okay. You guys play with your toys." I hugged them and went back into the living room. Dick was lying in wait for me. He grabbed the cocktail table, which had a glass top, and threw it at me. Immediately it shattered. Upon impact with my body, the glass cut both of my legs. He then attacked me repeatedly, beating me from head to toe, using a stiff partial arm cast he wore on a sprained arm.

I felt sharp pains in my stomach and blood began to run down the inside of my thighs. The apartment security guard, Mack, hearing the screaming and commotion came to the door. Dick took off. He just left me there bleeding, on the verge of passing out. Mack picked me up. I went to my room and got cleaned up some. Mack got the kids, their clothes, and their Christmas presents together in bags. He helped me get into the car and drove the four of us to my mother's where we left the kids. Then he took me to the hospital. I was told I had just miscarried. I hadn't even known I was pregnant. They called my obstetrician, who arrived and performed a D and C. Dilation and Curettage is the scraping of the uterine lining to clean out the area after a miscarriage or other incidence of vaginal bleeding. Doctors also treated the cuts on my legs and wanted to check my face for nerve damage on one side. I had lockjaw and bruises from head to toe. I found out later that one of the doctors had called the police and reported it as a case of assault with intention to do harm. It seemed back then that domestic issues like that were not taken as seriously as they are today. In spite of the report, the police never contacted me.

The doctor told me I had been through a lot of physical trauma and wanted me to stay in the hospital for a couple of days. I told him, "No, I have to get back to my kids. I have to take care of them." The last time my children had seen me, I was all bloody. I didn't want them to think I was dead. I had to reassure them that their mommy was all right. He wasn't happy that I was leaving so soon, but left orders that I was not to lift my children or do any heavy work for several days.

A few hours later I signed myself out of the hospital. Mack picked me up and drove me to my parents'. I talked with Mom for the first time about the beatings. She encouraged me to go to the police. Because the hospital had filed a report, I was able to file charges against Dick for assault with intention to do bodily harm.

The police picked Dick up. I knew he wouldn't be in jail very long, though. At that time, I heard about many cases of men beating their wives. It seemed common in some circles of society. There were no laws granting the right to divorce your husband if he was in jail, nor were there laws against domestic violence. I realized that if I didn't do something, Dick would try and come back into my life as soon as he got out of jail. I hired a family lawyer and asked his advice. He drew up papers for an annulment since we were married less than a year and Dick and I had no children together. That would be a lot faster than a slower, court-granted divorce. Readily, I agreed. I wanted to make certain all ties were broken. The difficulty would be Dick. He had to agree to sign the papers. Somehow I had to convince him it was to his benefit to annul the marriage.

I went to talk to Dick in jail. Visitors were only allowed to meet prisoners in a visiting room with a glass partition between them. In addition, there were always guards present. I felt I would be safe. A prison guard stood nearby as I talked to Dick. I explained to Dick that I needed a divorce. As I expected, he refused. "No, don't divorce me, Anita. I'll change," he pled, giving me the same old song and dance.

I looked at him coldly, not believing a word he said, thinking only one thought: 'I want an annulment, and he is going to give it to me.' I didn't tell him that I had been pregnant and that he had just killed our unborn child. I'm certain that, in his mind, he had already justified the beating, thinking that I'd somehow deserved it. I knew that money was everything to Dick and I was convinced that was why he had married me. Money might be my ticket out. I told him the biggest lie that came to mind.

I said calmly, "You're in jail, unable to work. I have to go on welfare to take care of my children. If I don't, I'll have to give up the apartment. And the government won't give me money because I'm still married to you. They told me the only way I can receive financial help is if you agree to an annulment and sign these papers." He apparently didn't remember that I was getting some income from Social Security. I could tell that his thoughts were on any money that might be lost because of his time behind bars. It seemed he wanted money and would do anything for it. He looked at me and said, "Okay, I'll sign these papers. But will you marry me again when I get out?"

I smiled and lied through my teeth, "Of course I will." The guard gave me a look which clearly said he was angry that I'd ever agree to that.

Dick signed the papers. I took them and calmly walked towards the door. When I reached it, I turned around, stared at Dick, and said with all the contempt I could muster, "I wouldn't marry you again if you were the last man on earth!" The police officer gave me a big smile of approval and I left. Even though I had won, I was scared and shaking. I immediately took the signed papers to the lawyer and was granted the annulment. To help ensure that Dick could no longer threaten or attack me, I got a restraining order against him. For many weeks, he walked by my house, and often followed me. Every time he walked by, I was scared to death that he would beat me again. Weeks later, he finally left me alone. What a relief to end that chapter of my life!

I was ready for a *new* chapter!

7. From the Frying Pan into the Fire

After I was granted the annulment, I gave up the apartment. The kids and I moved back in with my parents. I took some time to recover emotionally, heal physically, and get back to basics. I'd never completed high school, so I took some classes at the adult school. I felt that counseling was needed, too - not just for me, but also for the kids. We had all been through such a traumatic experience. We were stressed and on edge.

I made an appointment and went to the counseling office recommended by the social worker. The moment we stepped into the waiting room I got a feeling from head to toe telling me I needed to leave right away; just take the kids and leave. This was not the place for us to be. It just didn't feel 'right'. I sensed something bad might happen there. There was no feeling of calm or comfort, both of which we all desperately needed. The look on the kids' faces told me they weren't comfortable either. They sat in the waiting room chairs slumped, almost curled into little balls. That was not the way they usually behaved in doctor's waiting rooms, so things didn't seem to feel right to any of us. I listened to my feelings and we left. I never tried to make another appointment there, or at any other counseling agency. I coped as best I could, answering questions the kids asked as honestly as I could, telling them as much as they could understand at their young ages. Linda was almost five years old and Miguel was almost two.

Mom knew about some of the abuse, but it would be difficult for me to talk about the situation with anyone else, especially a stranger. And, knowing how protective Dad was of me and my children, I couldn't bring myself to tell him. I didn't want to remember or think about the frightening and painful violent moments. It was just too soon. It was also embarrassing that I had allowed myself to get into that position and put my children in that type of environment. I had worked so hard to be responsible, to always do the right thing, and to be a good parent.

Mack, the security guard from the apartment building who had taken me to the hospital, came to the house several times to check on us. He seemed concerned and acted like a gentleman. He wanted to make sure there were no other problems. One day he asked if he could take me out on a date. In a way, I felt obligated to be nice to him because he had saved me from Dick. So, I said yes. We dated on and off for a while. He had a full-time job, a decent salary, and he had been there for me when I needed help. He seemed to be a nice enough fellow. After Dick, I never thought I could trust men again, but after spending time with Mack, I thought I could trust him. When he asked me to move in with him, I agreed, but on the condition that he find a place big enough for the two of us *and* my three children. I didn't love him, but I thought he could be a good father figure for the kids and provide a more stable home life for us.

Mack found an apartment large enough for all of us, so the kids and I moved in with him. The moment I walked into the apartment a voice in my head shouted: 'GET OUT! GET OUT NOW!' I always felt I had angels guiding me. This time I thought I was just nervous about the change, so I ignored them and stayed. What a horrific mistake that was!

Once we settled in, I learned the awful truth. Mack was not the kind, caring person I thought he was. I soon found out that he was a heroin addict. To support his habit, he ran a house of prostitution and sold drugs. I knew this was not the type of environment I wanted my children to grow up in, but I didn't know how to get out of it. From the time we moved in, Mack tried to control me through mental abuse, just as Dick had tried to control me with physical abuse. He constantly reminded me that he had saved me and that I was indebted to him. He threatened that if I didn't obey him, he would make sure I did. He was a large, muscular man and I was intimidated by his size and strength. I found myself thinking 'How is it that I am once again in the same boat I had been in with Dick?' I guessed it was partly because I didn't listen to my inner voice, my intuition, or my instinct, and take heed. Now I would suffer the consequences. I wondered what toll this might take on me, and I worried about what might be in store for the kids.

Mental abuse can be as harmful and devastating as physical abuse, sometimes even more damaging. Mack was a master at it. It zapped all of my energy. I had experienced enough cruelty in my life already to know that I needed a plan, and I needed to get us safely away as soon as possible.

When I did not do as Mack wanted, he added physical abuse to the mental torture. Sometimes I would do things I really didn't want to do, just to avoid the abuse. He started doing drugs in front of the kids. I told him, "Don't do this in front of the kids. I don't care what you do to me, but don't do anything to, or around, my kids."

Not wanting to rock the boat, I told myself that I could deal with what was happening. As long as he didn't hurt the kids, I would tolerate almost anything. I struggled to think of a plan. How and when we could escape was the question. I didn't want my parents involved. I'd gotten myself into this situation, and someday I would somehow manage to get out.

Mack was addicted to heroin. He knew many people who worked in drug clinics run by reformed drug addicts where he could get methadone, another narcotic often used for long-term pain management. It is milder than stronger opiates and stays in the system longer. It is commonly used to help people addicted to heroin and other narcotic drugs ease off their usage by reducing what can be severe symptoms of withdrawal.[1] Theoretically, Mack could have treated his addiction by taking methadone. Rather than using it himself, however, Mack went from one drug clinic to another each day, getting doses of Methadone to sell on the streets. The money he made was used to satisfy his own addiction. After I moved in with him, he insisted I drive him when he made his daily rounds. I began to know the people who ran the clinics. Some of them asked me how I got involved in the situation. They said I didn't fit the usual profile.

I wasn't managing Mack's abusive behavior towards me very well and had not yet come up with a plan to escape. I coped the best way I could by doing what he asked. I numbed myself to the reality of the nightmare I was living. Mack never allowed me time to think or be by myself, so I had almost no time to form a plan. I knew what was happening was morally wrong, but at the same time I thought there was nothing I could do to stop it. I felt helpless.

One night, a spiritual experience gave me a forewarning. As I lay in bed next to Mack, lying there sound asleep, I completely froze. I felt pinned down, as though something heavy was physically holding me down. I could only move my eyes. From a dark corner of the room I saw a black shape rise from the shadows. It was an ominous, frightening image. Since I couldn't move at all, I felt trapped. It felt like the shape was choking me, and I couldn't talk or scream. It moved towards me, and I started praying. "God, please, please, help me. Please take this evil away

---

[1] Berkow, Robert, MD, Editor-in-Chief, *Merck Manual of Medical Information*, Home Edition, (Pocket Books, 1997), 488

from me." As I continued praying, I felt I could begin to move again. I was physically set free, but I was still very frightened.

I thought, 'I know I can't stay in this room anymore.' I slipped out of bed and went to sleep in the living room with the kids. The experience affected me for days afterward, and I never slept in that room again. I felt the house did not want us there, and that the spirit didn't like what Mack was doing to us. The spirit had sent me a clear warning. It was telling me to get out or I would be destroyed. I was more motivated than ever to figure out how to get away.

A few days later, probably in one of his drug stupors, Mack took me to the house of prostitution that he ran and raped me in the cruelest and most destructive manner he could. He not only raped me vaginally, but he also viciously sodomized me. It seemed that he thought he could do with me what he wanted. It took my self-esteem to an all-time low, and I thought the kids would be better off without me. I wanted to kill myself. But, I love my kids more than anything else. I couldn't leave or abandon them.

The next morning, Mack was shooting up heroin as if nothing had happened. I knew I had to leave before it started all over again. I couldn't continue living with him. I worried that he might do something to the kids, or try using them against me. I *had* to get away to save myself and my children. I thought, 'What do I need to do to get out of this? How can I run away?' Mentally, I organized an escape plan. The people I met at the clinics and Mack's parole officer from his former jail time had already been discreetly telling me to get out. At one of the office visits, the parole officer had slipped me a business card with his phone number. I hoped that at least one of them might be able to help me now in my moment of desperation.

I told Mack I was taking the kids to my parents. I knew they would be safe there. I confessed to mom, "Mom, I have to move back home with you and Dad." I explained to her how dangerous it had become for me with Mack. Mom was really shocked, especially when I told her I had thought about killing myself in an attempt to escape the cruelty.

I called the parole officer from my parents' house and told him how Mack had abused me. The officer asked if I wanted to press charges, but he said it would be better not to. What he told me next chilled me to the bone. He warned, "He will never leave you alone. You know that. I'm not going to go into details and tell you why he was in prison, but you may never get away from him. You may never be safe."

Filing charges didn't matter to me as much as escaping from Mack and this brutal life of repeated torture. I didn't want to continue living in fear for myself or the kids. I was tired of living a nightmare.

"I will leave him," I said firmly to the parole officer. "Can you help me? Can you get him out of the house long enough for me to collect my belongings?"

"Yes, I can. I'll have to get a search warrant. But, it will only give you twenty-four hours to get your things out."

The next day the police arrived at the house with the search warrant, telling Mack that he might be in violation of parole. They took him into custody. An officer walked me to the back of the house and told me, "Your twenty-four hours starts now." I called everyone I knew who had a car, telling them I needed help. I needed to get out, and get out now! Within the hour, people arrived to help me remove furniture, clothes, and anything else we could pack quickly. We took everything we could back to my parents' house.

After about twelve hours or so, the parole officer called me at Mom's to say, "Be careful, I had to release him." I thanked him, reassuring him that I was in a safer place. He told me that he had ordered a restraining order against Mack, and it was my job to keep the restraining order active or I'd be in danger. Mack was not to come within a thousand yards of me and the kids.

I felt safe at my parents. A short time after we moved in, I learned I was pregnant. I prayed that the baby would not be affected by the physical trauma and the stress of everything I was going through. The gynecologist asked if I wanted an abortion. I told him firmly, "No, it doesn't matter. I'm having this baby. No matter what happens, this is my child."

After a short recovery period, I began to work again, doing home interior parties, multi-leveling marketing, and selling Jewel Tea. These jobs taught me how to judge people's buying habits, and to notice the ways they react to different marketing techniques. I tried to go forward with my life, but, despite the restraining order, Mack would come to my parents' house. We knew better than to let him in. He had learned I was pregnant. I talked to him through the window, trying to convince him it was useless to pursue me. "You will never know who this baby's father is," I said firmly. "Just go away, and leave us alone." I was determined to protect this baby from him. As far as I was concerned, he would never have the opportunity to influence this child's life or put them in what I considered to be an unhealthy environment.

When I was seven months pregnant, I met Jack. He moved into the house next door with his brother. He was twelve years older than me, and a Mariachi musician. I often went over to visit Jack's sister-in-law Marie. She was very nice, and her children got along well with mine. We became friends.

I was cautious about men now more than ever. This time, I knew some of the young man's family, which made a difference in my opinion of him. When Marie told me that he was already living with someone, at first I wasn't sure she was right because he had been paying so much attention to me. When I asked Jack and he admitted it was true, I quickly told him I didn't want any further contact with him. I knew what it felt like to be cheated on. I did not want to be "the other woman."

During my eighth month of pregnancy, I came down with chicken pox. I was covered from head to toe with red blisters and was very sick. My parents took me to the emergency room where they put me under quarantine because chicken pox is so contagious. Since I was pregnant, there wasn't much they could do for me. They put calamine lotion all over my body and sent me home to rest. While in the ER, the medical staff gave me a scare. They thought the chicken pox might have harmed my baby. The virus that causes chicken pox is one of the herpes simplex varieties. It can be very dangerous for babies because it can go to their brain and cause irreparable damage. I was already concerned about the baby's health, now to hear the chicken pox might also cause problems was more than I could bear to think about.

Two weeks later, I went into labor at home. My father couldn't take me to the hospital, so Mom called Jack. I wasn't too happy about that, but I needed to get to the ER quickly. When hospital staff assessed the situation, they found that the baby was in trouble. As a "blue baby," the umbilical cord was wrapped around her neck, and she was not getting enough oxygen. To add to this, she was in a breeched position with her head up instead of down in the birth canal. Her feet were presenting first. With the cord wrapped around her neck, if they tried to pull her out by her feet, the cord would likely choke her. Her arms might spread open and cause the skin around my vagina to tear. I could bleed out. It was too late by then to do a Caesarean. They had to act fast.

Because Jack had taken me to the hospital, the staff assumed he was my husband. Since this was a life or death situation, they asked him if it was necessary, who should they save: me or the baby. To this day I don't know how he answered, but my gut feeling is that he chose me because I was already a mother to three children and they needed me. Who knows, maybe he just wanted to make sure he could keep me around for his own personal reasons.

I was connected to an IV, a heart monitor, and who knows what else. They gave me shots of some sort, so I was not fully aware of what they were doing. The doctor took a chance and used both of his hands to turn the baby in the canal so that she would be in the head down position. In the process, he also had to pull the placenta downward to keep the cord from tightening and choking her. There was a risk in doing that because it might cause the placenta to separate from the baby too soon. If that happened, it could block the birth canal and suffocate the baby.

Due to the skill of my obstetrician and our own will to live, the baby and I *both* survived. Alyssa came through the delivery unharmed and appeared to be a perfectly normal, healthy baby. I was so relieved! I was allowed to see her for just a few minutes in the delivery room before they moved her incubator to the nursery.

My doctor told me that while they were sewing me up, he had difficulty stopping the bleeding and they almost lost me. He strongly advised that I *not* have any more children. I was just twenty years old, so they considered me too young to do a tubal ligation. I would have to be careful not to get pregnant.

Since I had gotten the annulment from Dick, I had chosen to go back to using Paul's last name. Since I hadn't legally married

Mack, I assumed my new baby would carry Paul's last name also. The next day when they brought Alyssa to me, I was surprised to see that they had put Jack's last name on the baby's bassinet. Even though I had told him I didn't want to be with him, Jack continued to let the hospital think he was my husband and the baby's father. Maybe he thought I would change my mind and want to be with him, or that I would *have* to be with him for the baby's sake. I really didn't know what his intentions towards us were. When I asked the hospital staff if I could correct the last name, I was told "No." I didn't want to open a bigger can of worms, so I didn't persist, and Alyssa left the hospital with Jack's last name on her birth certificate.

From the minute I held her in my arms, I knew that, like my other children, she was a gift from God. To add to the sweetness of this birth, after all the drama which preceded it, she was a beautiful baby.

Given that this baby had Jack's last name, I assumed he planned on being in her life. Now I felt obligated to try to get to know him better. We dated for six months. Then Mack reappeared. He was still suspicious and wanted a paternity test to find out if she was his baby or Jack's. He threatened that he would take her away from me if he tested positive as her father, and swore he would destroy me. I feared that Mack could ruin Alyssa's life with his addictions and what I believed to be an immoral lifestyle. I felt keeping him out of her life completely was the *only* way to protect her. I shuddered with fear and apprehension when I imagined what her life with him would be like. I refused the paternity test.

I was fearful that if I left Alyssa with anyone else for even a little while, Mack would take her and I might not see her again. I took her everywhere with me. I was even worried that he might take my other three children just to hurt me, so I took them with me most of the time, too. It wasn't always easy, but I felt it was something I needed to do.

I found out that Jack's second cousin lived nearby and knew Mack. He reported my every move and told Mack what a darling little girl Alyssa was. Mack's friends and the women who worked for him made my life miserable. They followed me and would say, "That's Mack's kid."

I would say, "No, she isn't," and walk away.

Mack continued to harass me: "I will destroy your life."

"Not if I have a say in it!" I would retort.

I had been telling people that I would never get married again. Mack knew that. I decided to tell him that Jack and I were going to be married. Mack's response was, "If you're really getting married, the baby must be his. What man would want to raise another man's child?" It's amazing what people can rationalize when they are looking for answers. I was surprised that my tactic appeared to be working.

I agreed to marry Jack to continue the façade. The ceremony took place at the Justice of the Peace six months later.

Mack *finally* left us alone.

8. Party after Party....

When Jack and I were first married, my mother was very ill with diabetes-related health issues, and Dad had a serious heart condition. They needed someone to care for them and to help with Rocky, so we continued to live with my parents in their old Victorian home. Downstairs there was a large basement which we converted into an apartment. There was a kitchen, a bathroom, and a living room that doubled as a bedroom. We kept Alyssa's crib in the kitchen. Linda and the other two kids shared a large bedroom upstairs with Rocky.

I stayed home and took care of my parents and the kids. Jack worked occasionally in his brother's auto body shop next door to our house. Before long, Jack and I began to live separate lives. Jack spent more time with his brothers than he did with our family. They constantly partied, drinking and staying up all hours of the night. Jack continued to play in the Mariachi band. They would be gone for hours, sometimes all weekend. For some reason, I wasn't welcome in that part of his life.

I thought Jack's brothers avoided me most of time because I would stand up to them and put them in their place. Sometimes when they ran out of food or drink in the middle of their party, often after midnight, Jack would wake me up and tell me to go to the store or to cook for them. I wasn't about to become anyone's servant, so I told them I wouldn't go. They could just get what they wanted for themselves. A couple of times I put dog biscuits in peanut butter sandwiches, so hopefully they would notice and not ask me to cook for them again. They were so drunk they never noticed and just ate the sandwiches and kept playing their music. One of his brothers, Manuel, was nice to me. Uncle Manuel, as the kids called him, played with them and was a big help to me.

I got the distinct impression that one of Jack's sisters didn't care much for me. I didn't understand why she didn't like me, but I did know that she and Jack's mother criticized me behind my back. Her husband, Morgan, on the other hand, was very kind and understanding.

One day close to Thanksgiving, we went to Irene and Morgan's for a family thanksgiving dinner. I was standing on their front porch, ready to leave. When I turned around to say good-bye, I felt a hand reach out and push me hard enough to lose my balance. I fell down the six concrete porch steps. Somehow I managed to get up, but I didn't feel well. Shaken by the fall, I said my good-byes, and we went home. I was two months pregnant. When I got home and started to bleed heavily, I knew from previous experience that I was probably having another miscarriage.

Jack was half drunk and didn't seem to care about what was happening. As for my parents, I didn't want to trouble them when they were both so sick. I didn't go to the hospital and just passed the baby there in the house. I assumed my body would heal itself, so I didn't go to the doctor. But, within a few days I became very ill. I had a fever and a migraine, felt nauseated, and my body was trembling. This went on for days until I realized I should make an appointment with my obstetrician. He examined me and saw that the miscarriage hadn't been complete. A part of the fetus was still inside my uterus. He did a D & C and, for the second time, warned me, "Physically you are able to have children, but your body is tired. You really should stop having babies. With all the physical abuse you have gone through, you need to be careful."

"But, I want one more son," I said.

"You shouldn't have any more children," he insisted. "Just

be happy with the family you already have!" He reminded me that I had almost died giving birth to Alyssa. "I don't want to tie your tubes yet because you're so young." (I was only twenty-one years old and a tubal ligation would throw my hormones into a very early menopause.) "You should consider preventing further pregnancies. Your body just can't take it." I didn't want to hear that advice and chose to ignore it. I got pregnant again.

Jack continued to party with his brothers every weekend and play in the Mariachi band. In different ways, we needed each other. He needed my financial support, and I felt I had to stay with him to protect Alyssa. I thought as long as he wasn't a mean drunk, I could manage.

As my parents' health improved, we moved from their home to a house across town. The move out of the neighborhood would also reduce the odds that Mack would bother us. Jack started working at a local winery. How convenient for someone who drank so regularly to work at a winery!

When the landlord raised the rent on that house, we needed to move again. Jack's cousin, Lenny, told us about a house across the street from him that was available for rent. Because he knew the owners, they allowed us to move in without paying the typical last month's rent and deposit. We only needed to pay the first month's rent.

Life wasn't easy at home. We didn't have much money, and even with Jack's paycheck, it was difficult to pay bills. We had almost no food. For several months, we ate corned beef hash from cans the Rescue Mission gave us. There are maybe a hundred different ways you can make corned beef hash taste halfway decent: hash and eggs, hash burgers, hash with barbecue sauce, hash with syrup. You name it and we've probably tried it!!! After three months of eating hash, I felt like saying "Forget it!"

Linda was in elementary school, another child was in a preschool nearby, the other two were still in diapers, and I was nine months pregnant. It was chaotic at home, and I had no help. One day while I was downstairs in the basement washing clothes, the kids were doing their version of "The Little Rascals," a television show from the 50's about innocent, but mischievous, children. My kids were getting into as much trouble as fast as they could. With me out of sight, they apparently thought they could do whatever they wanted.

I stopped loading the washing machine to listen for the kids. It was just too quiet, and instinct told me to go upstairs as quickly as a woman in her ninth month of pregnancy could. When I got there, I saw Alyssa playing with bottles of household cleaners from under the kitchen sink, some of which were toxic. As I grabbed her from the floor, I heard Miguel's voice outside; just as cars were driving by. I dashed outside and brought him in. Then I heard the toilet flush and saw my preschooler in the bathroom. They had sprinkled cleanser all over the floor and toilet. Green powder was on their clothes and in their hair. I got them out of the bathroom and used the vacuum to get the cleanser off because I was afraid if it got wet, it might absorb into their skin.

Upset, and not knowing what else to do at the moment to get things under control, I used scarves to tie two of them to a chair, and tied Miguel to the end of the bed. I wanted to keep them all safely in one place, clean up their messes, and get a handle on the situation. As soon as I had them settled with the scarves, I sat on the floor and cried. I was frightened thinking about what could have happened if I hadn't come up from the basement in time. I was feeling alone and overwhelmed. The kids started to cry, too. We sobbed together.

Just then, Linda walked in from school. She saw her brother and sister secured by the scarves, and could see we were all crying. She asked, "Mommy, what's the matter?"

I couldn't answer her. I was thinking, 'How could I have lost control this much? I'm a terrible mother.' I rationalized that I needed to do *something* to make sure they were safe! I was feeling very inadequate.

Doing the only thing she knew to make me feel better, Linda came over and gave me a big hug. With a soft little voice she said, "I love you, Mommy."

The good cry along with Linda's hug and "I love you" helped calm me down. I untied the kids and asked them, "Are you kids going to be good now?" They nodded their heads yes. The rest of the afternoon we sat quietly in front of the television eating popcorn together. I wanted them to know that I had been worried about them and loved them very much.

I sure learned a lot from that experience! After that, I made sure the bathroom door stayed closed as often as possible, and I put all the cleaning products downstairs in a box, labelled and out of reach. Kids don't come with an instruction manual. As a young parent, I just had to learn as I went along.

Soon after this incident, Jack's brother Manuel needed a place to stay for a while, so he moved in with us. The kids were really happy Uncle Manuel was there to play with them, and I was happy to finally have some help. One morning I was mopping the floor with a vinegar cleaning solution and Manuel was making breakfast. My water broke. Jack wasn't home, so Manuel piled the kids and me into the car and quickly drove to the hospital. My feet smelled like the cleaning solution, so when I was being admitted to the emergency room, the nurse asked, "What did you do? Did you take a vinegar douche before you came here?" I explained that I'd been washing the kitchen floor when the water broke.

I was taken to the labor and delivery room. They inserted a tube between two vertebrae in my lower spine so that they could give me Caudal Epidural injections to eliminate the pain from the contractions. Five shots seemed to have little, if any, effect. They couldn't give me any more. I was in full-blown labor by then, and could feel each sharp contraction. The pain was intense, but I managed to deliver a healthy baby boy. I saw him before he was whisked away by the nurses.

I was in trouble, however. Nurses whisked me off immediately into surgery. I was told later that they had to give me several blood transfusions because I was hemorrhaging. The doctor was finally able to stop the bleeding and saved my life.... again. After the anesthesia wore off, I was told that he had also cut, tied, and cauterized my fallopian tubes to prevent further pregnancies. I wasn't upset with him. He had warned me twice before not to have more children, but I hadn't listened and was happy that I had been able to give birth to one more son. This doctor had treated me from 1967 until 1975, had safely delivered all five of my kids, and saved my life three times. I knew he had my best interests at heart. I knew I should trust his judgement call this time.

While I was in the hospital, Jack's brother Manuel took care of the other children at home, giving them breakfast in the morning, driving the two older ones to school, and even cleaning house for me. I felt like Manuel did more to take of the kids than Jack did!

It was December 22nd and I wanted to be with my kids on Christmas Day. I prayed to the Virgin Guadalupe, "Please, let me go home to be with my children on Christmas Day." My prayer was answered and I was allowed to go home on Christmas Eve. The hospital sent the babies home in Christmas stockings in recognition of the holiday. Dale looked so cute! We celebrated the day with Mom, Dad, Rocky, and the rest of the kids.

The following months became one of the most difficult periods in my life. I'd just given birth to my fifth child and was working hard to take care of all the kids plus keep the house going. We were invited to a friend's house in Monterey for New Year's Eve. At the party, a woman named Gloria took an interest in me. She was friendly and we had some good conversations. When she learned I was married to Jack, she said something that caught me off guard. She said to keep my eyes open, and that if I ever needed anything, I could call her. I didn't know what she meant at the time and just thought it was a bit odd to say something like that to someone you just met.

The guys decided we should stay overnight since they were too drunk to drive and they wanted to continue playing their music. I called Mom, who agreed to keep the kids overnight, and we stayed. Gloria and her husband lived about a mile away from the party and invited us over for breakfast the next morning. We had a wonderful visit, and I got a chance to get to know Gloria better. I never wanted to have a girlfriend because in the past I never had good luck with them. They had either cheated on me, criticized me, or otherwise stabbed me in the back. Most were totally unsupportive. I was still cautious with Gloria, but somehow I felt this time things might be different.

A few weeks later, Jack went with the band to Monterey again, this time to play at a wedding. I got an anonymous phone call that Jack was with another woman. I was determined to keep the marriage going to ensure that we would be protected from Mack. When Jack returned from Monterey, I told him about the phone call and confronted him about what the person had said. He said *he* wasn't doing anything; it was the woman who was all over him. He wanted to know who had called me. Even though I recognized the voice, I told him I didn't know. He was persistent and kept asking, but I wasn't about to give up my source! I made it clear that I was not going to tolerate him being with another woman, and I was not going to give him a divorce. He needed to behave as a responsible married man and father.

For the most part, I felt Jack just wanted me to pay his bills, support his party habits, and, like the other men in my life to this point, to be at his beck and call. I wanted to show him that I was more than a banker or house keeper, and that I could fit into his world, too. I didn't really want to become a party person, but it seemed it was something I could do to keep our marriage going. It would also help me keep a closer eye on him. I told myself, as if I was saying it to Jack, 'You want a party person? Just stand back and watch!'

9. Can Things Get Any Worse?

I lost some weight and managed to get down to a size five dress by walking and running with the kids, and watching what I ate. One of my sisters-in-law encouraged me to learn the band's songs so that I could sing with the Mariachi band. Of course, Jack didn't like that idea. He could no longer leave me at home with the kids and party on his own as if he were single, nor could he easily fool around behind my back.

I drank some alcohol, but, I was responsible and kept it to a minimum. I wanted to fit into Jack's party world, but I did not want to risk being irresponsible with my kids, or lose them due to alcohol-induced stupidity.

That summer, we went with Jack's cousin Lenny and his new wife Terry to visit Jack's friends and relatives in Arizona. Linda was in school, and our preschooler wanted to stay with Grandma, so I left them at home with my parents. We took Alyssa, Dale, and Miguel with us. I learned on that trip that Lenny was close friends with Mack. I worried that somehow spending time with him might lead to further contact with Mack, and I really wanted to avoid that. I went into defensive mode.

Alyssa was eighteen months old and cute as a button. When we arrived at Lenny's, most of the adults were starting to drink. The other children there were not being supervised, so I decided to look after all fifteen kids. It wasn't much of a vacation for me!

Lenny was captivated by Alyssa. He kept looking at her. Finally he said, "I think she's Mack's child. He should see her."

I bristled. I told Lenny, "You don't know who her father is. Neither does he. If Mack shows up, there will be trouble. There's a restraining order against him. If he comes near us, I'll be forced to call the police. Please don't encourage him to come see us."

We returned home safely enough from Arizona, but I was worried. Would Mack show up in the neighborhood and, even worse, come to our home? What would I do if he did? Would the police protect us? There were too many unknowns.

When we came back from Arizona, it seemed more than ever that Jack expected to be at the top of our family's priority list. It became especially evident one day when I had to pick Linda up from school. School wasn't out yet and Jack called, wanting me to come pick him up from his job at the winery before getting Linda. If I drove to pick him up first, however, I would be late getting to Linda. To Jack's way of thinking, she could wait. I knew that if I wasn't there to pick her up soon after school was out, Linda would walk the eight blocks to get home. It was getting dark and I worried about her getting home safely. Half-way to the winery I thought, 'He can sit and squat for all I care! I have to get Linda. She's only a child! *He* can wait.' I turned the car around and went back to the house. There she was, my little seven-year-old daughter, sitting forlornly on the front steps waiting for me. I was glad she was safe and that I had decided to return home before getting Jack.

Linda and I left for the winery. True to form, when we arrived Jack was madder than hell. He blew up at me, yelling and screaming at the top of his lungs.

I told him, "You know my kids come first. I told you when we married that you would always be second." He didn't like that. He thought *he* should always come first.

Soon after that incident Jack lost his job at the winery. He was upset and took off to go drink with his brothers. By then he had become verbally abusive with me. When Jack was sober, by all appearances he acted well enough with the kids. But, when he was drunk he would get after them, sometimes for no reason, and make them kneel on bricks as punishment. One time Alyssa came to me after being punished and asked if she had to kneel on the bricks because her daddy loved her. I told her no, it was because she had done something she wasn't supposed to do. I hugged her and said *that* is how people show love. I was not into physical punishment. I would send them to the corner and tell them to stop and think about what they had done and why. We'd talk about it after their time out. I tried to get them to see how their behavior or words could affect other people and understand that is why they were being reprimanded. That method of discipline seemed to work well in our family. The kids sure remember that corner!

Jack drank more and more as time went on. Money began disappearing from the house. I couldn't pay the utility bills or hospital bills from Miguel's tonsillectomy and Linda's surgery to enlarge her bladder. We were in debt. I had to go to the Rescue Mission again to get food, clothes, and other things we needed. That was very difficult for me. I thought I'd left the hard times behind. The only good thing about the situation is that I used it as an opportunity to teach the kids about money. I told them about our bills, counted money with them, and tried to teach them about budgeting and how to make what little money we had go farther.

As the drinking and the finances worsened, my trust in Jack dwindled even more, and our relationship fell apart more each day. We were constantly at war with each other. The kids felt the tension, too.

I heard that Mack had been to Lenny's house across the street. I didn't know if Mack knew we lived on the same street or not, but I panicked and felt we needed to move away.... and move quickly. We had nowhere else to go, so we lived in our station wagon for almost a month. Thank goodness it was during the summer and the weather was warm. We literally set up camp on Mt. Madonna, past the picnic areas so that no one would be as likely find us. We slept in the station wagon because the raccoons came out at night. All we could afford was an occasional cow head, which we cooked in a metal drum that we buried in the ground. It was cheap and would feed us for a few days. It was windy sometimes, so we built a wooden lean-to for protection, especially while we were eating. We built an outhouse with boards and branches that we found in the area. We took showers at Mom and Dad's. I didn't want them to worry, so we just told them that the pipes were being worked on at the house to explain why we didn't have water. Our resourcefulness paid off. We had a great view from the mountain, and we survived for thirty days or so there.

By the end of the month, we moved into a rundown apartment in East San Jose. The apartment was literally bug infested. We stayed a couple of months until the city heard of the condition. Just before the holidays, they gave all tenants thirty days to vacate the building before condemning it. Merry Christmas! Again, we had nowhere to go.

At the same time, Mom was seriously ill and in the hospital. She had bumped her foot some time before, but never said a word about it until green lines went up her leg. It had become infected and cells were dying off. Gangrene had developed. The pain was severe. Doctors told me that with her advanced diabetes, any injury or surgery would take longer to heal and be more life-threatening. They felt the only thing they could do for her was to amputate the leg. They transferred Mom from the hospital in San Jose to UCSF to perform the operation.

At age eighty-two, with a history of multiple heart attacks, Dad's health was declining also. He no longer drove on freeways, so I took him to see Mom every day. Mom wasn't doing well and was not up to signing papers. Dad could not read English and spoke very little of the language, so I signed papers on Mom's behalf. Signing the consent form for the amputation of her leg was one of the most difficult things for me to do. But, without that procedure, they said she could die within a few months. I had no choice.

The surgery took much longer than expected. After several hours, the doctor came out to tell me Mom would need to be in the intensive care unit longer than they had anticipated. It would be touch and go for the next twenty-four hours. They advised us to go home and get some rest, saying they would call us if there were any changes.

One time I was in the room when they changed the bandages. She was obviously experiencing intense pain. I held her hand and asked God to please give me her pain. He must have heard my prayers, because after that I could feel her pain so much that I nearly passed out. One of the nurses caught me as I was fainting and sat me in a chair in the hallway. When they had finished changing the bandages, the doctor came out and mentioned that they would need to be changed several more times over the next few days. They requested I *not* be in the room when they did it. I felt badly about not being there to support Mom, but it was also a relief. I hated seeing her in such pain. It was almost more than I could bear.

After several weeks in the hospital, Mom was moved to the rehab center where she would get physical therapy and learn how to work with her prosthetic leg. I was so relieved and happy that her condition was improving! It was quite a process putting the new leg on and learning to walk with it. The pain got to Mom, so she continued to take pain medications. They seemed to make her quite groggy and that delayed her progress some, but we didn't want her suffering either. It was just going to take time.

Dad and I went to see Mom in SF every day. Alyssa, Miguel, and Dale stayed with my cousin in San Jose. I left the other two kids under Rocky's care. Rocky could fix them sandwiches, and they would sit down in front of the television to watch the daily kid shows. I gave the kids strict instructions to mind their Uncle Rocky and stay near him. With his mobility issues, he could fall. They needed to understand that he could get hurt. One rule: No chasing around the house! They did as I asked and were very good with him.

As a mother, I always wanted to spend quality time with my kids. Looking after them, taking care of Dad, and seeing Mom in the rehab facility daily, it was challenging to find the time, but I was determined to do it all. I wanted to be Super Mom. Sometimes it was as simple as talking with them while fixing their breakfasts and lunches, cleaning their ears, or combing their hair. When there was enough time, we all sat around the coffee table and I read the *Bible* to them, answering questions as we went along.

The Rescue Mission gave us a lot of clothes, which we received after we sat through a religious service with local homeless people, many of whom appeared to be like the winos portrayed in some movies. On one of those days, we were lucky enough to be given ten bags of clothes and blankets. I decided to take them to the laundromat to wash them before the kids wore them. To add to my responsibilities that day, I had two of my girlfriend's children with me. That meant there were seven children, ages two and a half to nine years old. I still always wanted my kids with me so I could know exactly where they were and with whom. It was difficult to keep track of them while tending to the laundry, but I was determined to get it all done. Dale and a couple of the other smaller kids got into the huge dryers and started to run inside them. Dale thought this was a great way of getting attention, and kept yelling, "Look Mommy, look!" I had to go rescue him when one of the other kids thought it would be funny to close the dryer door on him. *I* was not laughing.

Frustrated with trying to keep track of all those active kids inside the laundromat, I decided to put them in the more confined space of our station wagon. The windows were open for ventilation, and it was parked right in front where I could see them. I thought it would be safer to have them there than scattered about the laundromat, and I assumed I would be able to keep an eye on all of them at once while I tended to the laundry.

The laundromat was located on one of the busiest streets in East San Jose. While I was filling the washing machines, one of the children climbed into the front seat of the car and began experimenting with the car's control levers. They didn't know what they were doing. They were just playing with whatever knobs and levers they could reach. They took the emergency brake off. The car didn't move. Then they fiddled with the levers around the steering wheel. All of a sudden I saw the car start to roll out toward the busy intersection. I couldn't believe my eyes! The way the parking lot was, the car was parked on a bit of a slant, so it rolled easily. One of the side doors was wide open. As the car rolled back, Miguel fell out the back window, landing on the drainage grate that was in the lowest part of the parking area. One of the car tires ran over him. The car slowly went through the parking lot and rolled to a stop in the middle of the intersection. It was amazing the car didn't collide with any other vehicles!

It was happening so fast! I couldn't get there soon enough.

Panicking, I immediately ran outside. A stranger, seeing what was happening, ran into the intersection and pushed the car back into the parking lot, then called for an ambulance. Another person advised me to wait for the ambulance to arrive instead of moving Miguel right away because we didn't know what his injuries were. They could become even more serious if we moved him ourselves.

The police and an ambulance arrived, and the paramedics examined Miguel. He was taken to the emergency room at the nearest hospital. The kids and I followed the ambulance in the station wagon. While we were in the waiting room, the police talked to me and seemed ready to charge me with child neglect. I was crying and surrounded by the kids, and told the police what had happened. The kids were crying, tugging at me, saying, "Don't take my mommy!" They told the officers I was a good mommy. The police decided to let me go, and left the building. Just after they left, one of the kids got my attention to let me know that three-year-old Dale was intending to pull the fire alarm in the emergency room. Boy, did I run fast to stop him! Good thing I wore my running shoes that day!

When the doctors came out after examining Miguel, they told me he had a punctured lung and that it was amazing he didn't have more injuries. The grate in the parking lot had actually saved his life because it dropped him lower than if he'd just been on the level concrete. The car had rolled over him rather than crushing him. The doctors said he would need to be in intensive care for at least seven days with a tube in his lung to keep it inflated. Mom and Miguel were in different hospitals in two different cities. I was at my wit's end, feeling over-whelmed and like I just couldn't handle any more.

As if that wasn't enough stress and drama, when I got

home later that afternoon, nine-year-old Linda told me something that made me feel sick with rage. She said, "Mommy, I have to tell you something." Linda was an avid reader and always looked for new things to learn. She even read every word on each page of a dictionary! That day she had come across words that made her think about some things that had been happening to her. They lead her to realize it was inappropriate behavior. She proceeded to tell me that Jack had been molesting her. I had only to look at the frightened expression on her face to believe her. As I heard more, I found out she sometimes took his abuse in order to protect her younger siblings. She didn't want them to be hurt, too. I was livid.

I thought to myself, 'You can harm me, but you cannot hurt my kids!' In my shocked and outraged state, I wanted to hurt Jack as much as he was hurting Linda. I rushed to the hall closet and took out his Colt 45 pistol. If I shot him where it counts, maybe he would no longer hurt my daughter. Jack was at his usual place, his brother's. I wanted to get him immediately, and didn't want to have to explain anything to Dad, so I took the kids to Connie's. I explained to her what had happened and asked if she would please take the kids to my parent's house for me, adding, "I'm going to go shoot Jack."

"You know," she warned, "If he presses charges against you, he could end up with custody of all the kids." I paused and considered what she said. In all the years of her trying to influence my life, this time she was right. I was married to Jack. And with my parents in such poor health, he would get custody of the children if I was arrested. I wasn't going to let that happen!

I put the gun away and called our family pediatrician to ask for an appointment for Linda. I explained everything to the nurse, and they told us to come in immediately. After the exam, the doctor told me, "It doesn't appear there has been any loss of virginity. But, that doesn't mean he hasn't molested her. The mere fact that Linda agreed to the examination is all the evidence I need. I'm going to have to call the police and child protective services."

I said, "By all means, please do." I believed Linda and thought the police or protective services would keep Jack away from my children, some place where he couldn't harm them anymore.

The police did call Jack into the station for questioning, but soon released him. I was stuck. Jack would still be living with us. I found a place for Linda to stay temporarily where she would be safe. Alyssa and Dale were with one of my cousins. I asked her if she would please keep them for a few days while I was going back and forth between the hospitals in San Jose and San Francisco to check on Miguel and Mom. Fortunately, she said yes. She and Connie now knew about the suspected molestations, but I told no one else.

Child Protective Services sent two of their agents to the house a few days later. Linda bravely explained that her stepfather had been doing things to her. The agents didn't believe her and accused her of making it all up. One of them was more specific and vocal about it. He said he thought it was just a matter of her not wanting me to be with *any* man. In his opinion, maybe she thought if she made up a story like that, Jack would have to leave. Then she could have things back to the way they were before. The agent was literally blind and couldn't see the expression on her face as she was telling them about the incidents. I believe he was unable to get the whole picture.

Since the agents didn't believe Linda and saw that the pediatrician's report was technically inconclusive, they didn't feel there was sufficient evidence to prosecute Jack, much less have him investigated. The police and Child Protective Services were apparently not going to be able to help me. Their hands were tied, too. I was stuck in a situation that I worried could be potentially dangerous for all of my children.

I later thought about how brave Linda was to let me in on Jack's secret. He had told her that if she told anyone, he would kill me. It takes a lot of courage to go against that kind of threat, as well as a lot of trust between mother and daughter. As an adult, Linda wants to encourage anyone in that kind of situation to please tell someone, anyone. Try to get help. Healing from the emotional damage that can result from being molested takes a long time. Some of the effects can impact the rest of one's life. The faster one can get away from that environment, the less potentially damaging the effects may be.

The legal system was not going to order Jack to leave the house. Jack reminded me that he is Dale's biological father, and made it clear he had no intention of moving out.

What a month that was! With all that going on, we were supposed to find a new home, too. It was getting near the end of the eviction period. We were almost out of time! I needed to find another place to live quickly, even if it meant Jack going with us. We had been in Section 8 housing before, but the income reports they used this time included Jack's salary at the winery. He had made just enough money that we were one dollar over the limit to qualify now. They were not willing to bend the rules, even though it was so close. I managed to find a house to rent, but I couldn't afford the required deposit or first and last month's rent. Dad came to my rescue and got a loan so that I could get into that house.

Miguel was released from the hospital shortly after we moved. It was so close to Christmas and people at the loan company knew I was having a hard time. They took up a collection in their office to buy presents for my kids to open on Christmas Day. They even gave us a canned ham for our holiday dinner. I was very touched by their generosity. The Salvation Army had a Christmas program where the kids could go to a big party and get a gift from Santa. I always wanted the kids to have a happy Christmas, so when I heard about that, I signed up right away. Overall, I think the kids had a merry Christmas.

Early the next year, Mom was released from the rehab facility. I stayed with her at her house for a few days to help out. The pain from the amputation was still intense. The whole situation was very difficult for Mom, and hard for me to watch. With the pain medications, she was incoherent and not always aware of her surroundings. Sometimes she punched and hit me, not knowing what she was doing. They say people who have had amputations still sense the limb is part of their body. Mom didn't sense her leg was missing, or remember that she only had one leg, so she would try to get out of bed. This put her at a high risk for falling. Waking up frequently throughout the night, she needed to be watched closely. The caregiving job was made more difficult because the hospital had neglected to order a hospital bed in time. It would have railings to help keep Mom safely in bed. Instead, for the first three nights I had to restrain her with a special vest from the hospital. That upset Mom, but it was the best way to keep her from falling and getting hurt. I was relieved when the hospital bed arrived on Monday.

When the medical case worker came to assess the situation, she ordered a home health nurse to help with in-home care. Rose was sent to work with Mom. Her caring attitude and physical help was such a blessing for us. She stayed during the day, and I slept by my mother's bed at night. The daughter of

Mom's best friend relieved me for one night, but it was too much for her to handle. Exhausted after that one sleepless night, she confessed, "I don't know how you can handle it, Anita." Neither did I, but I felt a sense of responsibility to take care of my parents. I remembered all the things they did for me growing up, and the love they showed me. I thought of all the Wednesdays spent either going to the movies with Mom, or to a wrestling match or roller derby with Dad. Spending time with us, no matter what we were doing, was one-on-one quality time with each of them that I truly appreciated even more as I grew up and had my own children.

As the year progressed, Mom continued to recover and Miguel was getting better, so some things were looking up. I was still stuck with Jack, though, and worried he might hurt Linda again or do something to the other kids. I told him I wanted him to move out. He threatened to let Mack become involved in our lives again. I felt I had no choice but to let Jack stay at the house. I didn't let the kids out of my sight. Everywhere I went, they went.

I warned him, "You are nothing but scum. If I find out you did anything to any of my kids, I'll report you to the authorities. I'm warning you, don't push me."

I've got my eyes on YOU!!

10. A Normal Year .... Almost .... The Calm Before Another Storm

Life the next few months almost had a sense of normalcy. It was 1977 and a new year. Miguel's injuries from the incident in front of the laundromat had healed, and we had celebrated a reasonably happy Christmas. We were finally in a home large enough to accommodate a family of seven. I had signed a year lease for a change. That felt *so* good! It seemed we could finally settle in somewhere permanently. I could enroll the kids in school, and they could begin friendships that could last for more than a few weeks or months. It felt like a fresh start for all of us .... except possibly for Jack. He avoided being home much of the time, which was fine by me because it gave me a break from feeling like I had to keep my eye on him the whole time.

I loved our house. The lay-out was so roomy, and there was a good-sized yard for the kids to play in. The house had been decorated by an Italian family who had put beautiful green and burgundy tiles on the kitchen and bathroom walls, from the floor half-way up toward the ceiling. It was so easy to clean, too. What a great time-saver with five children in the house! There were other conveniences, too. The washer and dryer were on the same floor, near the kitchen. It was so much easier to keep track of the kids and still get household chores done.

One of Jack's friends from the Mariachi band frequently came to visit. One night he had a bit too much to drink and began telling me all his personal problems. He was not happy. He told me how much he admired that I was so caring and always put family first, always trying to do the right thing, even if sometimes it didn't come out that way. He also liked that I was strong enough to stand up to Jack. He knew things were not great between Jack and me, and suggested I leave Jack to find someone who would appreciate me and love me for who I am. He told me Jack didn't know what a good thing he had. It was a bit awkward, but it was nice to hear that someone appreciated me as a person and was supportive.

Our home became a place for both of our families to gather during the summer. There would sometimes be ten to fifteen people at our house along with the Mariachi band. The band would practice for hours in the back yard. Their music must have been enjoyed by the neighbors because, much to my surprise, even with the late hours, no one ever complained or called the police. We always served a lot of food, and the kids had their cousins to play with. Those were fun times.

One evening, Hal, one of my cousins from Mom's side of the family, came over to visit. Usually he only came over after he'd been drinking. He said he was on his way home and wanted to stop by because he had heard that we had the Mariachis playing at our house every so often. That night they were not there, and I was home alone with the kids. He asked for something to drink, and as he didn't seem to be drunk, I gave him the last bottle of beer from the previous party. He must have already had a few drinks before coming over, though, because his behavior changed. He started talking loudly and making advances toward me, which I naturally refused. I told him to leave. He said he needed to use the bathroom first, so I said ok, but he was to leave right after that. Telling him to leave angered him, and instead of going to the bathroom, he went to the boys' room, grabbed Miguel, and locked him in a choke hold. Dale, who was in the crib, began to cry. Miguel was calling "Mom, Mom…" I ran to the bedroom as fast as I could, and when I got to the door, I could see Hal holding a large pocket knife to Miguel's throat.

At that point, I told him I would do whatever he wanted. "Just don't hurt my son." As he moved the knife away from Miguel's throat, I was able to silently reach the 45-caliber revolver hidden on the top shelf of the hall closet right next to the room. I didn't know if it was loaded or not, but I pointed it at him and told him, "I'll shoot if you don't leave my house right now!" I could tell by the expression on his face that he was surprised. He started coming toward me. I told him the gun was loaded and I was not afraid to use it. I could tell the police it was self-defense. As he walked toward the front door, I walked behind him every step of the way. I pushed him out the door with the gun at his back, then slammed the door shut and locked it. I yelled to Linda to lock the back door, called 911, and put the gun back in the closet. When the dispatcher answered the phone I asked them to have an officer come immediately. I told them there was a man outside our house who had just held a knife to my six-year-old son's throat. When they arrived, they quickly arrested Hal. I was glad they took him into custody before taking time to ask a lot of questions. He might have gotten away.

After the police took Hal off, the kids and I sat together watching TV to calm down and let things get back to a sense of normalcy so we could go to sleep. What a nightmare it had been!

Hal never visited again, and the months passed quickly. Soon it was Christmastime again. My dear friends Stewart and Gloria came to help us celebrate the holiday, with Stewart dressing up as Santa Claus for the party. Remembering how I had felt left out at Christmas gatherings at Connie's home, I made sure to have extra gifts for unexpected guests. I always wanted everyone to feel included in the festivities.

A couple of years earlier, Stewart and Gloria had been so kind as to propose they would buy me a house in Monterey next door to them. They had also offered me a job in their freight business. I truly appreciated their offers and kindness, but I declined both offers because I valued their friendship more than material things. I didn't want to risk losing that relationship if things didn't go according to plan. It would also have been difficult moving so far away from my parents. They were the only people I felt I could truly trust to take care of my kids while I was at work.

Almost exactly one year after moving into the house, Mom called to ask if I would move back to their house to help take care of Dad. She was doing better, but his heart condition was getting worse, and it was more than she could handle, even with Rose's help. I hated to leave the home we had been settled into for the past year, but my parents' needs had to take priority now.

11. A Shot in the Dark

We gave up the house and moved back in with Mom and Dad. Mom needed more help now because Dad was having multiple heart attacks. When someone is having a heart attack, quick action is required to save their life. With Mom's prosthetic leg, she was unable to get on her feet quickly. Rocky did not know how to use the phone. We developed a plan to deal with the emergencies so that we could get Dad to the hospital as soon as possible. There was a buzzer in my parents' bedroom that we extended so that I could hear it downstairs where I slept on the couch. When Dad was having a heart attack, Mom would ring the buzzer, I would call for an ambulance and open up the yard gate and the front door. While waiting for help to arrive, I'd try to keep Dad as comfortable as possible. It got to the point where emergency services didn't ask for the address any more. They already knew because I'd called so many times and they recognized the phone number.

In October, 1978, with the seventh heart attack since I had moved in, the doctors decided Dad should have emergency open heart surgery. When the operation was over, they came to us in the waiting room and told us the surgery hadn't gone well. They didn't know how much longer Dad would live, and advised us to go be with him in the recovery room. Mom and I were at his bedside when he looked up at me and, with his eyes looking into mine, said, "Good-bye. Take care of your mother." As he passed away, Mom held his hand. I think she knew, as I did, that it was his time to leave us. He'd been through so much the past few years. We were so glad we had celebrated his eighty-fourth birthday in June with a big party. Jack's brothers and the Mariachi band provided music and entertainment. Many friends and family members were there to honor him, and I think Dad enjoyed it.

During the first days after Dad's death, Mom and I called relatives and friends, and planned the funeral. Most of the family, including Dad's sons and grandchildren from Mexico, attended. The service was in a Catholic church. We talked about his many accomplishments during his lifetime, and shared memories.

Mom needed my help now more than ever, learning to live without Dad and dealing with her own health issues. Fortunately, we still had Rose's help with physical care during the day. Mom and Rocky moved downstairs to the smaller living area so that the kids and I would have more room. We each had our own kitchens and living quarters.

Jack was still living with us. I wanted him to leave. Every time he left to spend time with his brothers, I hoped he would stay with them. But, like a bad penny, he always returned. After Dad died, Mom and I pooled our money to make it easier for me to pay Mom's bills as well as mine. Besides the mortgage, utility bills, insurance, and medical supplies for Rocky and Mom, there were daily living expenses like paying the milkman, the bread man, and the produce man who all delivered food to the house. Sometimes Connie requested money, too. The only income we had was Mom's Social Security and Paul's survivor benefits for my first three children. My widow's benefits had stopped once I married Dick. I had been going to beauty school in hopes of graduating and getting a job as a beautician. I only needed to pay for two hundred more hours, but Jack made me quit. He wanted me to be home more, or so he implied. He wasn't working either. As I think about it now, I really wonder if the issue was that he didn't want me to have more education than he did.

With no earned income and a large family to support, we needed financial assistance, so I applied for welfare benefits for

Alyssa and Dale. Jack was not very happy about that. He did *not* want any part of the welfare system. But, what else was I supposed to do? He wasn't working and we needed money.

I felt I had to keep my eye on Jack every day to keep my kids safe from him. The stress weighed heavily on me, both mentally and physically. It seemed the only way to get Jack out of my mother's house was if *I* left. I arranged to pay Rose a bit more to stay with Mom and Rocky, and left my contact information with them. I took the kids and ran away twice, intending to come back to Mom's after Jack moved out of the house. Somehow he always found us. On my third attempt, the kids and I went to a town near Fresno to stay with some of Dad's relatives. I thought we might have a better chance if we were further away.

I never wanted my children to be without an education, so I registered them at the local school. What I didn't realize was that Jack could locate us through the registration information. After two weeks with my nieces and nephews, Jack found us yet again. That was how he found us the other times, too. I didn't want to cause a family scandal, so I hadn't explained to Dad's family why I left Jack. I didn't want the rest of the family to feel obligated to get involved, or try to rescue me. When Jack showed up, we were forced to go back with him. I told Jack I was returning for Mom's sake, not his.

During the short time I was gone, Jack moved a gal named Penelope into the house. She was sixteen years old. He introduced her as his daughter. He had never mentioned to me before that he had a daughter! She had apparently been living in another state, so I guess he hadn't felt the need to tell me. I assumed he had asked Mom's permission for her to move in, but found out later that he hadn't. Penelope acted resentful of me. She claimed I had taken her father from her.

From what I saw over the next few weeks, it appeared they did not have a typical father-daughter relationship. The two of them spent a lot of time in the garage together. It seemed a bit odd. I wasn't the only one who noticed. One night as I was walking to a neighbor's house for a visit, I saw Jack sitting in the front seat of the car with Penelope. When I got to Natalie and Dan's, Natalie said, "Anita, I don't think that's his daughter. They aren't acting like father and daughter!" She thought she saw them making out in the car, and told me I should confront him.

Rose mentioned noticing some other behaviors, too. I confronted Jack, who tried to explain that after not seeing Penelope for a long time of course they wanted to spend a lot of time together now. I didn't believe him. Spending time together with one's children doesn't mean making out with them! He felt that he had taken in my kids, so I should take his daughter in, too. I reminded him that I would turn him into the police if he tried any funny stuff – if, indeed, Penelope was his "daughter." After all, he was thirty-nine years old and behaving like a teenage boy with a girl of sixteen? It seemed odd to those of us observing them.

Dan and Natalie wanted me to forget about Jack and enjoy myself. They suggested I go out with them. "You just need to have a little fun," Natalie said.

I told them, "I don't want anybody. I'm beginning to hate men! I'm literally sick of them!" But, I remembered something that made me think. My girlfriend Jennie knew a Chinese astrologer. Just a few weeks earlier, she had given him some information about me, and he had done an astrological reading. He told her that I would have terrible times ahead, but that I would get a divorce and remarry for the last time. If I chose wisely, that marriage would be a good one.

I was surprised when Jennie reported what the astrologer told her. "Me? Get married again? I don't think so! I've had enough!" But I didn't forget the prediction.

A few days later, Dan and Natalie invited me to a CB Radio get-together at a community center where they introduced me to Arnold. He was about thirty-two years old, cute, and treated me very respectfully. He treated me like a person, not a possession. We danced a few times and before I left he asked me to go out with him.

I was twenty-seven years old at the time. I wanted to be honest with him, so I told him, "I can't go out with you. I'm still legally married, and I have five children. I'm also taking care of my mother and brother." He thought that I was pretty cool, and liked that I was honest and open with him. I told him, "I'll bring my children to the next CB social event, so I'll see you then and you can meet my kids."

When Jack got wind that I had been out dancing, he confronted me. I reminded him of the times I had caught him with other women, and of his highly suspicious behavior with Linda. I told him, "I'm not like you. I did nothing wrong."

"Are you going to go out again?" he asked.

"Yes, I am. And I'm going to take the kids with me." The club always offered fun things for kids to do while the adults were socializing. While I danced, the kids were occupied and had a good time. They saw Arnold and me dancing. They said nothing about it because they knew how much I love to dance. We were all happy being away from the stressful atmosphere at home.

One evening when the kids and I got home, Jack was in the garage with Penelope. They were drinking. Remember, Penelope was only sixteen, so not of legal age to be drinking. It also smelled like they were smoking something besides cigarettes. I opened the garage door. It seemed that something was unusual, and possibly inappropriate. I looked at the young woman he called his daughter and realized that their behavior was definitely *not* what I would call typical or appropriate for what he claimed was a family connection. Thinking back to what Natalie had observed, I questioned more and more who Penelope really was. I shuttered to think he was behaving that way with his own daughter, but I really didn't know what was going on.

I told Penelope, "You need to get out! I don't want you in my house. Why don't you go to your grandmother's house down the street? You're *not* welcome here! I don't want my kids around you." Penelope didn't say a word, just put her head down and went into the house.

Jack got very angry. He said I had no right to kick her out. He went into the house and got his rifle, then sat down in the big chair in the garage. He continued drinking heavily. Penelope left and went to her grandmother's house, but not before saying she was going to find a way to separate Jack and me. My response was, "Thank you. It would be great if you could do that!"

I was beyond caring any more. Living with him the past six years was worse than being in prison. I told him, "You know what? You can sit there and sulk for all I care! I don't care what you do! I just don't care anymore! Whatever you do, just don't leave a mess!" Then I went into the house and started to put the kids to bed.

One of my cousins was staying with us at the time. She was downstairs in the basement with half the kids, and I was upstairs with Mom, Rocky, and the other kids. Suddenly, we heard shots being fired in the direction of the back yard.

'Awww, I hope he didn't miss,' I thought coldly. I thought maybe he was drunk enough he might attempt to commit suicide.

Then, I thought, 'Wow! Now I've got to clean up *that* mess!' At that moment I really hated him.

I got into bed and prayed, "Dear God, I don't know how I'm going to get out of this mess, but if it's meant for this marriage to Jack to end now, give me a sign. Have Paul's family come and see my children." I had not seen them in years and didn't know where they were, or what had become of them. As far as I knew, they knew nothing about what had become of us. It would be a miracle if they contacted us. That would be my sign from God.

Next, I heard a second set of shots. I got up to go check on everyone. Fearing the worst case scenario that I might be accused of assault or murder, or just firing a gun, I went to the garage, opened the door, and saw Jack sitting in the chair. The only comment I could muster up was, "Oh, you're still here. You must have missed!"

He replied, "I'm not going to miss this time!" He fired three shots in my direction. I ran into the house with him at my heels, rifle in hand, and making a lot of commotion. Barbara ran up the stairs, using hand gestures to discreetly ask if I was okay.

I looked at her, shook my head slightly and mouthed, "No, not okay." I didn't want her to get hurt, and I worried that Jack would hear us or see us talking. Quietly, I whispered, "Get the police."

Jack then pulled the telephone off the wall and proceeded to pull the ham radio wires apart. I had run back outside. Jack ran to the car, opened the hood, and removed the coil to the distributor cap so that I couldn't start the car if I tried. At this point, it seemed I was trapped. I wanted to check on the kids, so I ran back into the house. Barbara sneakily started to crawl down the driveway to get help. Jack, who had by now followed me back into the house, heard her. "There's someone outside," he said.

I denied it. "No, there's no one there. Are you getting paranoid or what?"

I'd had enough. If one of the bullets hit and killed me, he might end up with my kids, and I *really* didn't want that! I couldn't just sit there and let him terrify me. I had to distract him so that Barbara could go call the police. I told him, "You want target practice? I'll give you target practice! Let's go outside and see how fast I can run! I bet I can outrun your bullets!"

Jack was distracted just enough that Barbara made it to a neighbor's house and called the police. In no time, six police cars pulled up in front of the house. Four officers came around the back, and two stayed in front. They knocked on the front door. Jack looked at me and said, "You were able to call the cops?"

"Are you stupid? How was I supposed to do that? You pulled the phone out of the wall. You see me standing here in front of you. How could I have done it?" Then I proceeded to use every foul, four-letter word I could think of to throw at him. I was at the end of my rope with him and didn't care what I said.

The knocking at the door became more urgent. "Don't answer it," he ordered.

"If I don't answer, they're going to think something really is wrong. So, either you let me answer the door, or shoot me right here. Either way, let's get this over with!"

I rushed to answer the door. The police took one look at me and noticed the look of sheer panic on my face. They pushed me aside and came into the house. Jack ran out the back door still holding the rifle in his hand. The police caught up to him, pinned him to the ground, and cuffed him. He was on his way to jail and I might be free of him, at least for a little while.

One of the officers who stayed behind after Jack was hauled off to the police department, informed me that even after catching Jack with the rifle, they would have to report this as a domestic dispute rather than attempted murder. In the 70's, it seemed the police did not get involved in cases of domestic violence. A woman could call for help after being beaten by her husband and the police could do nothing. Unlike today, there were very few shelters where women could go to escape. The officer told me, "We have him in temporary custody for now, but we'll have to release him soon. It would be wise to make other arrangements for your safety."

The police were going to release him? I knew I was in serious trouble. Jack would be madder than ever when he got out of jail. I went back into the house and was able to reconnect one of our phones. Immediately I called Rose and asked her to please come take care of Mom and Rocky, telling her I had to take the kids and get away from the house as soon as possible. She arrived at 2:00 AM. I got the kids dressed and called Dan and Natalie to see if they would come pick us up.

"Please, come get us," I begged them. "Jack just tried to kill me. He's at the police station now, but the police told me they might have to release him tonight. Since you just moved, Jack doesn't know where you are living now, so I think we may be safe staying with you temporarily."

"Okay," said Natalie, we'll be right there." It didn't take them long to arrive. Just then, an officer from the police department called. They warned me that they would be releasing Jack within the hour. I knew he would come back to the house. He would never hurt Mom or Rocky, and Rose was going to be there, so I thought they would be safe. I left, not knowing when I'd be able to return.

The kids and I stayed with Dan and Natalie for a few days while I waited for things to cool down. Because of what happened before when we tried to get away, I knew that if the kids went to school, Jack would find us, so I home schooled them while we stayed there. With Natalie and Dan's three children, there were eight children and three adults living in one small house. It was crowded, but we managed.

To repay Dan and Natalie for their kindness, I did all the cleaning and helped with the cooking. I also gave them some money to pay for the extra groceries. I left Natalie's phone number with Rose so she could keep me updated about Mom's health. We'd been there for about ten days when Rose called. "Your mother is very sick. You need to do something. She's very worried about you."

Mom and Rocky blissfully and amazingly didn't know what had happened with Jack. Mom was heavily sedated with the medications she was taking and was unaware that I had come so close to being killed. Rose couldn't remain at the house indefinitely. I knew I had to return home, but, how could I go back there, knowing Jack would be there?

I went to the police department and got a restraining order against Jack. He was not allowed to come within 1,000 yards of me or my children. Jack finally had to move out.

Once I obtained the restraining order, I went home. Rose met me at the door, telling me that Jack's daughter Penelope had moved in again while I was gone. I went to Penelope, yelling, "Get out of my house! I told you before you're not welcome here!" I walked Penelope back to her grandmother's house. While there, I told Jack's family that he had not only tried to kill me, but I suspected he had hurt my daughter. I no longer cared about scandal. I was going to tell them everything. He deserved no sympathy. No surprise, they didn't believe me.

The Ballistics Division from the police department called a

few days later. The bullet had only missed my head by six inches! Jack was shooting to kill! It was a miracle that I wasn't killed! I wasn't going to risk another incident like this. Next time I might not be so lucky. I went to Mom's lawyer to file for a divorce. He said because it was a domestic dispute, the only reason I could file was irreconcilable differences, which he said were unquestionable. Jack could not challenge me. I did exactly that.

I felt my life changing. We were going to be free of Jack, and I no longer felt so alone. Rose, Natalie, and Dan were good friends who supported me. I was able to care for Mom, Rocky, and my kids.

My Godfather Randolph called around that time. His wife had passed away a few months earlier, and the rest of his family lived far away. He asked if he could stay with us if he needed a place to live. I hesitated for a moment because I didn't know if I could take on another responsibility. But, I knew he had helped my mother in previous years, so I said "Yes, of course, you're always welcome."

If you recall, a few weeks earlier I had asked God for a sign that it was time for this marriage to end. I had prayed, saying if it should end to please have Paul's family come see us. It seemed like a miracle. They *did* come to the house! Paul's mother, two of his sisters, and his brother knocked on the front door one day. I'd not seen them in seven years. Somehow they remembered where my parents lived and came to get my address. They said they were just stopping by to see how we were doing. I was so surprised. The visit was very brief. After seeing the kids, they left. I never saw them again. My mind was more at peace after their visit. I felt reassured that this divorce was right in God's eyes.

I needed Jack to sign the divorce papers so I could go on with my life. He didn't want to sign them at first, but I told him I was sure I could get proof that he tried to kill me. I could send him to prison. He decided to sign the papers.

We still had to go through a custody hearing regarding Dale and Alyssa's future contacts with Jack. Naturally, after the suspected inappropriate behavior with Linda, I was very nervous that Jack might get partial custody of Alyssa now. I feared for her safety and well-being. My lawyer presented the earlier report by Child Protective Services. Jack's attorney countered with the CPS agent's report that stated he did not believe there was any truth to the allegations of child molestation. I couldn't believe the judge would take a chance and grant custody in favor of Jack. But, he did. Jack was granted visitation rights for both children.

Alyssa never wanted to be close to Jack or go places with him. Whenever he came to pick them up, she would kick and scream. I usually told Jack, "Just leave her here and go! Remember to bring Dale home early. I don't want him out late." Dale didn't seem to mind going with Jack, probably because there was less supervision at his house, so he could get by with a lot more than he could at home. Jack did as I requested. He knew I would not hesitate to follow through on my threat to press charges of attempted murder if he did anything to harm my kids. It was like I was on a mission. I was going to protect my children and myself, no matter what it took. I was numb, as if I'd become hardened. The only feelings I allowed in were for my kids, Mom, and Rocky.

12. New Beginnings

It was late 1979. The kids and I were still living at home with Mom and Rocky. I knew they needed me more than ever after Dad's recent passing. Mom was doing much better health-wise, so Social Services cut Rose's hours to fifteen hours per week. That meant the rest of the time I was solely responsible for Mom and Rocky's care.

Looking for a job at this point was out of the question. With Jack out of work, I knew it would be nearly impossible to get any child support from him. Fortunately, I was still getting Social Security Survivor Benefits for three of my children, and welfare assistance for the other two. Mom was getting similar Survivor Benefits from Dad, and Rocky got Disability benefits. We had income, but we also had the mortgage on the house and large bills still owed on Mom and Dad's medical expenses. I had to budget very carefully.

Coincidently, my Godfather, Randolph, called me again. He was not in good health and told me he was unable to live alone any more. He had sold his home and did not want to move to a care facility. He asked if the offer to live with us was still open. He would help with monthly expenses in exchange for living with us and receiving some caregiving. I agreed, with the condition that he would have to share the one upstairs bathroom with all of us. With all the people I was responsible for at home, it took some planning and coordination to get him moved and settled into our house. He had already gotten rid of many of his personal things, so we managed the multiple trips on the twenty-five mile drive from his home to ours in just one weekend. It really was good timing for us to have help with the finances. Maybe it wasn't really coincidental timing? I believe someone was looking out for us.

I converted our front living room into living quarters for Randolph. We closed the big double doors between the living room and the dining room so he could have some privacy. We made the dining room into the living room for the rest of the family. That lead to using the kitchen for our dining area, and it wasn't big enough for all of us to sit together at meals. We more or less ate in shifts. Cooking was quite a task as it was with Mom and Rocky's diabetic requirements. Randolph had his own dietary needs, so that was another consideration. Overall, though, he was pleasant and kind, so it worked out well enough.

It was a good thing I had a big station wagon to take Mom, Rocky, and Randolph to their doctor appointments! I couldn't leave anyone at home, so everyone went for the ride regardless of who had the appointment. This went on for several months until one afternoon at the house Randolph appeared to have had a stroke. I called an ambulance and he was admitted to the hospital. They needed a blood relative to help with his information, and to sign release forms. The hospital called his nephew, but he lived too far away to come on the spur of the moment. When Randolph was ready to be released from the hospital, his nephew had enough advance notice that he could pick him up. Before getting Randolph, he came to my house to ask me to take care of his uncle. I told him I had as much as I could handle with Mom and Rocky's disabilities, plus taking care of my kids who were all under twelve years of age. His response was to say that he'd pay me. I told him I was sorry, but that no amount of money could give me the energy and time needed to give the quality of care they all needed and deserved. I packed up Randolph's belongings and gave them to his nephew. He seemed upset that I didn't take his offer to pay me, but I had to do what was best for my family. I occasionally needed some time for myself, too, and that was hard to come by already.

Going into the next year, Mom's health was doing much better, four of the kids were in school, and Dale was gone part of the time in preschool. Social Services said they would increase Rose's hours again if I had a job and would not be home as much. I could finally work. I found an eight-to-five job at a farm supply store. I carried fifty-pound sacks of animal feed, dispensed syringes filled with antibiotics for horses and cows, and cleaned out the incubators for the baby chicks. Sometimes I manned the cash register as well.

The supply store was a family-owned business. One of the sons would hit on me, thinking he could get away with it and not risk losing his job. He displayed an attitude of arrogance and was quite demanding. He thought I was out partying every night because I was often late getting to work in the mornings. The real reason was that Rose was often late, and I couldn't leave the house until she got there. In addition, there were no sexual harassment laws in place to protect working women, so I was forced to smile and try to ignore various comments with innuendos. To say the least, that didn't make my job any easier. There were always snide remarks as the workers passed by me. Customers would enter the store and I had to act as if nothing unpleasant had happened. Some, however, knew how the sons were. When the men bothered me, I told them I had a boyfriend, even though I didn't.

With the security of having a job, I went to the social worker in charge of my file to see if there was some way I could get off welfare assistance. "How do I do it? I want to stop getting assistance and don't want to depend on welfare anymore. I have a job now, but there are a lot of expenses and I just can't make it yet financially without help. I hate getting the welfare checks because

I know there are people who need them more than I do. I'll really be in trouble if you cut me off too early, though. Please, help me get off the rolls."

The social worker was in his thirties and must have understood how I felt. He agreed to help me, but only if I promised not to tell anyone how he was going to do it. He told me, "Don't report that you are working for the first month. The next month, report that you are working. They'll still send a check for that month, and your last check will come in on the beginning of the third month. After that, I must terminate you." With that amount of time and the extra money I thought that could work. The social worker wished me luck, and I left his office.

Before the last check arrived, I took all my receipts in to show him that the money I had been given had gone toward paying off all the debts that had accumulated. I managed to take care of my children and pay off my ex-husband's pile of bills, as well as take care of my parents' medical expenses. I wanted to reassure him that his kindness had genuinely helped me. At the time, I was supporting eight people. On my own, I never had enough money to pay for everything, no matter how hard I worked. I appreciated the extra help from social services, and I never went back on welfare again.

I started to date again, but because I didn't trust men, I didn't let any of them get close enough to hurt me. Past experiences had taught me to be careful. When I was on a date, I always had money in my pocket to help me get home, and a phone number to call in case I found myself in trouble. I had no desire to be tied to one person, and I enjoyed my freedom.

I continued to go to the CB community gatherings with Arnold. On weekends, Barbara and I went dancing at some of the local discos where I met several interesting men. I met Kent when he asked me to dance. He was Mexican-American and acted like a gentleman. We went out on dates a few times. Then I met Glenn. He was very wealthy. After dancing we went out for a late dinner at an upscale restaurant where I met some of his friends. They were a snooty crowd. He thought he could impress me with his money. I didn't care how much money he had, show-offs did not impress me. I didn't go out with him again.

There was also Jay, but he was much younger than me. I was his first love, and he worshipped the ground I walked on. He was very family oriented, and on many dates we took his five nieces and nephews and my five children to the movies or the park. He was very sweet, but, I was very cautious.

In the Fall of 1980, with all the responsibilities I had and having just gone through a divorce, I knew I needed to get a handle on my emotions. I started going to group therapy meetings. There I met Sophia. She had ended her marriage because she didn't like her husband any more, not because she had been abused. I thought that was odd. I had never heard of anyone divorcing just because they no longer liked the person!

A lot of the people at the therapy meetings thought I was a floozy because at my young age of twenty-nine I had already been married, widowed, divorced, and had five children. I didn't let that bother me. At this point in my life, I didn't have time to think about what others thought of me. I had too many other things to be concerned about. I just wanted to be independent, self-sufficient, and to build a life my family and I could enjoy.

At one of our meetings early in 1981, Sophia said she had someone she wanted me to meet. She was on a bowling league and wanted me to meet her at the bowling alley later that night. I told her I already had a date with Jay, but she was insistent. Reluctantly, I gave in and said I'd go after I fed the kids.

As soon as I arrived at the bowling alley, I was introduced to Jerry, one of her teammates. He was Caucasian, thirty-nine years old, and, as I found out a bit later, he was married, but separated from his wife. He had a good job driving eighteen-wheeler trucks for a big oil company. I couldn't help but compare him to Jay. I looked at Jerry and thought, 'Jay is so much younger!' I felt safer with Jay, thinking I would not get attached to him due to the age difference.

I knew I was being superficial, but I was also being cautious. After bowling, Sophia asked me to go dancing with them. I loved dancing, and it was going to be a group activity. I didn't want to miss the opportunity, so I called Jay and broke our date. Jerry asked if he could drive me to the dance, and at first I told him no, but then I changed my mind. I said he could take me if he agreed to meet Mom, my brother, and my five kids first. I thought that condition would discourage him from wanting to ask me out by just seeing how much responsibility I already had. It was a surprise for me when he agreed!

He followed me home so I could leave my car at the house and check on the kids. He met my family and Rose. He said he'd wait on the front porch while I was getting the kids settled. I had a little time to freshen up for the evening. Linda, age thirteen, and her younger sister pushed him up against the porch wall and told him he had to be nice to me, or else. *That* was Jerry's introduction to my kids! Some men would have said "Hasta la vista!" at that point, but Jerry didn't.

We went to a dance club called Cowtown in San Jose and started to get acquainted by talking about our families. Jerry had been separated from his wife for over seven years, but neither had filed for divorce yet. His son Christopher, twenty-two years old, lived at home. His daughter Lynn was twenty. Her daughter

Brandy was just eighteen months old.

As the evening went on, no one from the bowling alley ever arrived. We figured out that Sophia had set us up on a blind date, and we both said, "Only Sophia would do something like this!" The music at this club was mostly country western, which Jerry really liked. He tried a couple of times to dedicate a song to me, but I kept walking away, not realizing the song was for me. I'd be in the bathroom or outdoors getting some fresh air. It was single's night, so there were dances that involved changing partners so that people could mingle. When it came to me, Jerry was eagerly waiting to dance with me, but I didn't recognize him, and just went on to the next dance partner. All in all, we had a great time.

There must have been a spark of attraction between us because at the end of the evening Jerry asked to see me again. I told him no, but then he asked if he could call me. I knew Sophia would give him my phone number anyway if he asked her for it, so I figured I might as well give it to him myself. I told him he could call, but that I probably wouldn't go out with him.

Jerry called several times during the next month. Each time I declined his invitation. Finally, one Friday night when he called, I said, "You're not going to stop until I go out with you, are you? I'm going dancing with my cousin, Barbara, but afterwards you can pick me up at two in the morning when the disco closes." I didn't think he'd want to go out that late. Then he asked if I wanted to go out for breakfast and meet some of his friends. So, I said, "Sure," still thinking he wouldn't show up.

As Barbara and I were leaving the disco at 2 AM, she looked across the parking lot and told me, "Look who's here!" To my surprise, there was Jerry! I gave Barbara the car keys so she could drive home, and I went with Jerry to Carrows for breakfast.

Later, when we got a chance to talk alone, I was open and honest with him. I told him I was going out with other men. Despite knowing there was competition, he wanted to keep seeing me.

One time Arnold asked me out, but Jerry asked me for the same time, so I told Arnold about Jerry and asked if I could bring him along, that he'd be good company. Being cool about it, he said, "No problem."

Jerry and I met Arnold at the radio club. The two guys began to talk and got along fine. The next thing I knew, I was left out of the conversation! They were like long-lost buddies who had been reunited. Having nothing better to do while they talked, I began drinking shots of tequila, one after the other, without counting how many I was drinking. Before I knew it, according to the bartender, I had downed twelve shots. The alcohol's numbing effects didn't hit me until later.

When the evening was ending, I said good-night to Arnold and told him Jerry was taking me home. He said that was okay and to have fun. Reassured that Arnold wasn't miffed at me, I prepared to leave the club. The minute I stepped outside, the effect of all those tequila shots hit me like a ton of bricks at the same time the wind did. I collapsed. Jerry carried me to his car and took me to his house, thinking it was better not to take me home in that condition. He was so good to me! He was a perfect gentleman and let me sleep off the effects of the alcohol.

It was four in the morning when I woke up. I told him, "I never do this." I explained that I needed to get home to be there when my kids woke up, no matter what shape I was in, and he drove me home. I got cleaned up, managed to fix breakfast for the kids, sent them off to Catechism class, and got to work.

When I got home that night, Mom asked if I liked Jerry. I told her yes, and realized I really did. We'd been going out for a month and he was becoming special to me. He was a good person, didn't take advantage of me or push himself on me, nor did he judge me on my past. He might be a keeper!

Soon after that discussion, Mom had a heart attack and was in the hospital. When she came home, she started to think about the future and what our lives might be like without her. "I know you're going to get married again," she said. "I know you will for the kids. But, I want to know: if Jerry asks you to marry him, will you?"

"Yes, Mom. I like him." That seemed to comfort her.

I prayed to God, asking him to please make Mom better. For a time, her health did improve. She enjoyed sitting with the kids and me. She was different from other mothers I knew. She and I were genuine and true friends.

After a couple of weeks, I talked to Mom about inviting the guys I was dating over to tell them I was only going to date Jerry from now on. She laughed and thought it was a great idea. I felt it would be safer to tell them in my own home. Before the other fellows arrived, Jerry showed up early for our date that night with a box of candy and a bouquet of roses. I answered the door with a towel around my wet hair. What a sight that must have been! I asked him to come back later, telling him that from now on I was going to be with just him, but I had some unfinished business to take care of first. He said, "Okay," and left.

The three guys I had been dating arrived at the house. I had always been honest with each of them. They knew I was not seeing any one man exclusively. They couldn't imagine what was going on that night and why I needed to see all of them at the same time. I stood in front of them and said, "I've gone out with all of you. Thank you for all the dances and the fun times, but, I can't go out with you anymore. I have been dating Jerry and we're getting serious. In all fairness, I have to let you guys go."

Arnold was great about it. He told me, "Jerry can give you more than I can. I'll always be your friend, but he loves you. I'm happy for you!"

Kent, on the other hand, got really mad at me. He had seen Jerry briefly, and his opinion was that I should stay within my own culture. I thought he was mostly after my money and wanted to control me. I told him, "It's your type I hate! You don't own me, you don't pay my bills, you don't take care of me, and I don't see that it is any of your business!" In a threatening manner, he told me he'd be watching me. I replied that I didn't care, he could watch me all he wanted. I would call the police if he caused me any trouble, even if I had to make up a story in order to get him away from me. He walked away and I had no further problems with him.

Jay, my youngest suitor, was so sweet. He sang a love song to me after the party. I think he was trying to convince me to keep seeing him. I told him he should find someone closer to his own age, someone who would love him for his kindness and for who he was, and not to give up on that.

That was it. I was ready to begin the next stage in my life… with Jerry!

13. REALLY???

One of the best ways to get to know someone is to see how they react in different situations, especially in my life. One afternoon in March, Jerry and I went to a local taqueria and were sitting in his car talking. At one point he called me "Kiddo," which really riled me up. I thought he was making fun of the fact I am almost eleven years younger than he. It made me mad that he was calling me a kid! I had worked so hard to be independent, and I wasn't going to let anyone make fun of me. I would not tolerate anything less than respect. I picked up my plate and told him I felt like throwing it at him. He didn't realize how upset I was by his comment, so he kiddingly replied that if I threw mine, he would throw his at me, too. I didn't want him to throw his plate at me because I was wearing a new dress and I didn't want it stained. He didn't want the mess in his new car either. We just both put our plates down, and I told him why I didn't want to be called "Kiddo." He told me he wasn't making fun of me and meant nothing negative by it. It was a term of affection. No one had ever used any terms of affection with me before! This was the first time I had a truly honest, calm, and reasonable discussion with *any* of the men in my life without the fear of consequences. It was the kind of open communication that I had always wanted.

Continuing with our conversation that day, I told him that I wanted him to be a part of my life with his eyes wide open about my past and the person I had become because of it. "I don't want anyone to walk up to you and say they know something about me that you don't already know. I don't have anything to hide, and I don't want you to ever look back with regret that you allowed me into your life."

I began by telling him about my childhood years, my

loving parents, and my precious few years with Paul. Then I spoke about my traumatic experiences with wife beaters, drug and alcohol addicts, and a child abuser. He heard about my close calls with death, including the deliberate attempt on my life. As the hours passed, I told him everything I could think of in a nut shell.

Years later, Jerry confessed that he almost couldn't believe everything I'd told him. It was all so incredible that so many things could happen to one person! He said what I was telling him didn't discourage him. He loved a challenge and still wanted to see me. One of the reasons he was attracted to me, I found out later, was that I was different from other women he had dated before. He had never dated anyone with a different cultural background. He once told a friend that he hoped I would teach him Spanish and about the Hispanic culture.

Since I felt more intensely about Jerry than other men I had dated, I wanted to see how my kids would react to him. He suggested we plan a day in the park. He asked what he could bring, so I told him to just bring soda and I'd bring the rest. The kids and I had lived so meagerly before, now that we had enough money I let them choose whatever they wanted to eat when we were out. We went shopping for the picnic, and they put shrimp, crab, Hebrew National hot dogs, potato and macaroni salads, chips, cookies, and what-nots into our grocery cart. When we checked out, there were at least ten bags of groceries. Jerry thought I'd bought out the grocery store! He declared that it was quite a feast.

While I set the food on the picnic table, Jerry played catch and soccer ball with the kids. We spent the whole afternoon at the park. He made a good impression on the kids. They really liked the fact he played with them. I was impressed that he really *did* spend time with them and not just me. I liked that! He seemed to enjoy the day with us as well.

With everything I'd been through in the past, I was more cautious than ever with Jerry. I didn't jump to any conclusions about him and where our relationship might lead. I wanted to get to really know him before considering any further or more permanent commitment.

I was somewhat bothered by the fact that although he and his wife had been separated for seven years, they were not yet divorced. I wondered if he wasn't over her yet and there might be a possibility they would get back together. I shared my concern with Jerry, and he reassured me, "No, I'm not going back to her, but I do have to pay alimony and buy out her half of the house that we bought together." His wife was working at an insurance company, but he still had to provide a significant amount of financial support for three years. These financial obligations, on top of his own expenses, were a big drain on his income. He had little money left for entertainment or unexpected expenses. Fortunately, his children were over eighteen, so he didn't have to pay child support. Both of them were working. Christopher was an auto parts manager and Lynn was attending the police academy.

Over the next few months, I saw Jerry as a calm, considerate, and gentle person. However, there was one incident that caused me some concern. He had received a letter that greatly upset him. He became angry and threw something in the bedroom. I was scared. I'd never seen him angry, and because of my past experiences with angry men, I was worried he might lash out physically at me just as they had. Lynn was with us that day, so I asked her if she thought he might hit me. She started laughing and tried to reassure me by saying, "No, he just gets upset sometimes, but he would *never* hurt *any*one. He just gets mad like everybody else."

'Oh, no, he doesn't,' I thought, recalling the beatings I had received in the past from men who had been "upset." I remembered vividly my trips to the hospital and the black eyes and bruises I had to cover up the next day.

I was still skeptical and cautiously observing, but Lynn was correct – Jerry calmed down, and things were fine within a few minutes. In all our years together, Jerry has rarely gotten truly angry, but when he has, the expression of anger is over in five minutes. The issue is over, done, and forgotten.

On another occasion, Jerry came to the house one Saturday. All the kids were home and playing. In our neighborhood and with all that we had experienced, I always tried to know where they were. Five-year-old Dale was often too curious and too smart for his own good. We were inside the house watching television, unaware that he was giving himself a private tour of Jerry's brand new car, a Honda Prelude. Dale came into the TV room and asked Jerry if he could play with the ball in his car.

"I don't have a ball in my car," Jerry replied with a puzzled look.

"Yes, you do," said Dale. "It's in your trunk."

Now concerned, Jerry asked, "How did you get into the trunk?"

At this point, we both got up to check the car. There were small footprints on the hood. Dale had climbed onto the hood and squeezed through the partially open sun roof to get inside the car. He pulled the back seat down, found the trunk release lever, and got into the trunk. A bit astonished by what had happened, Jerry calmly told Dale he couldn't play with the ball because it belonged to his son Christopher. I was embarrassed that Dale had gotten into the car without asking permission first, and told Dale that he had plenty of toys of his own to play with, so he didn't need to look for more. From that time on, Jerry kept the sunroof closed, doors locked, and the windows shut tight.

We went back into the house. With my five children, a bedridden mother, and a special needs brother, I wanted to know if Jerry thought he was up to coping with all the responsibility I had taken on. It was all a part of me. I asked, "Okay, you just had a little taste of what it's going to be like if you get more involved in our lives. Are you really ready for this?"

He answered honestly, "I don't know. It's been a long time since I've been around young children. Let's see how it goes."

I started hearing more from Jerry about *his* past one evening when, during a romantic candlelit dinner at his home, he got a phone call from someone in Oregon. I couldn't help but overhear the conversation. He was talking to a woman, saying he would see her when he was up there. I was taken aback. Who was she and why was he going to see her? I thought we were a couple, but it sounded like he was dating this person. When he got off the phone, I told him I would *not* play second fiddle to anyone and he had some explaining to do. He told me that June was actually his stepmother's daughter. He had been dating her off and on. Nellie, his stepmother, and her husband Freddie, had been good friends with his parents for many years. After Jerry's mother and Freddie died, Nellie and Jerry's father, Ron, married. Having known Jerry for a long time, Nellie hoped that he and June would form a lasting relationship. June's teenage children really liked him, too, and wanted him to become their stepdad. He told me he needed to go see her when he went to visit his father in Oregon, but that he would tell her they could no longer go out. I was still a little worried because they had been such good friends for so long. Maybe she or her children would convince him to stay with her instead of me? I soon found out I had nothing to worry about.

Neither of us was ready to commit to a more permanent relationship at this point, and we were cautious, but, we were both interested in each other enough to give it time.

Three months later, things were going well. We were more comfortable with each other, had developed a sense of trust, and wanted to spend more time together. We even talked about living together. There was a lot to think about if we wanted our relationship to grow. I tried to consider every aspect of our lives:

Jerry is Baptist; I am spiritual, but less attached to one particular religious sect.

He grew up in a "Beaver Cleaver" home very different from mine.

He is white American; I'm Hispanic American.

Jerry likes a structured household; I am flexible. My household ran with few rules; Jerry wanted rules.

There had been one wife in Jerry's life; I had been involved with four previous partners.

He had two older children; I had five young children.

I was currently not on a limited budget, but he was.

I put on big parties; Jerry did not.

He loved Country music; I loved Disco.

He loved to travel; I had never traveled.

There was eleven years' difference in our ages.

Jerry liked pet names for people he was fond of; I didn't care for pet names.

Obviously, we had many differences of opinion and different lifestyles. There was a lot to consider before we could commit to a more permanent relationship. I saw Jerry as a hard worker, a dedicated family man, and a caring person. He went with me to get damaged canned goods from local grocery stores to take to the battered women's shelter, something I had been doing as a volunteer for several months. That demonstrated to me that he had a giving and compassionate heart for others.

Jerry also had an adventurous, romantic side. I came to appreciate and look forward to his spontaneity. I really did want to get to know him better. Living together seemed the best way to do just that. We also needed to see which of us would compromise and adjust to our differences.

Once we made the decision to live together, we had to decide where to live: his place or mine. There were advantages to both places, but moving my mother, brother, and children was more than I wanted to deal with at the time. I asked my kids how they felt about Jerry moving in with us. Hands down, the kids said yes, he could move in, but they commented they were not ready for me to marry him yet. I wasn't ready for marriage yet either. We needed to see how things would be living together first. Jerry rented out his house in Cambrian Park and moved in with us in June of 1981.

Shortly before he moved in, Chevron promoted him to a new position in Concord, sixty miles from his home. Luckily for him, my house was eleven miles closer to his job! He had some vacation time coming, so, before he started the new position, he planned a trip to Canada and invited me to go along. I said yes, not realizing how far Canada was from California. Being a truck driver and traveler, distance was of little concern to Jerry, but it was a totally new experience for me! I'd never even been over the Golden Gate Bridge or traveled further than from San Jose to Reno, Nevada!

As I made preparations for the trip, making sure the kids, Mom, and Rocky would be cared for, I got nervous. Believe it or not, in all my years, I had never been further than a day's drive away from my children or my mother!

We started off on the trip. When we had driven about seventy miles, I asked, "Are we there yet?"

Jerry laughed and said, "No."

When we had driven approximately 200 miles, I said, "We have to go back home now so I can put the kids to bed." I trusted Rose and knew she would take good care of everyone at home, but it still felt uncomfortable not being there with them doing what I usually do every night. Jerry reassured me they would be fine, and we drove on. Around the 800-mile point, it was dark and I started to cry. I missed my kids. I wanted Jerry to take me to an airport so I could fly home. I had never flown before, so I would be nervous about that, but I wanted the fastest way home possible. He told me we were nowhere near an airport.

We stopped at a hotel for the night and Jerry encouraged me to call home. I talked to Mom and each of the kids. Mom told me to "Go, have a good time! You need this!" I wanted to read the kids a bedtime story. It was one way to reassure myself that everything was all right. It was part of my nightly routine. I guess I needed the familiarity as much as I thought my kids did. It was a long phone call, but one I needed to make. Jerry was very understanding and very patient with me.

The next morning, Jerry said, "We've come this far, let me take you on to Canada. Then, if you still want, I'll take you to the airport and you can fly home." I nodded yes and, being reassured by the thought of Mom's encouraging words, we continued. Along the way we stopped in Seattle, Washington, to have lunch at the top of the famous Space Needle. Jerry didn't know I am afraid of heights. He was disappointed I didn't get excited about it, but I was terrified the whole time we were up there and couldn't eat a thing.

Another new adventure arose when we took the car on to the ferry to cross over to Vancouver Island. I was scared because I had never been on water like that before!

Once on the island, we stayed in a quaint, thatched roof, cottage-type motel in Sooke Harbor. The scene might make you think of a Thomas Kinkade painting. The service was wonderful. We had breakfast served in our room, delivered by a person on horseback! It was a very romantic get-away.

Next we went to Victoria, staying in a Hansel and Gretel-type cottage near another one that had belonged to Shakespeare's wife, Anne Hathaway. The day we went to Buchart Gardens, I wore a long pink Victorian dress and we strolled through the beautiful acres of plants and flowers. He took my picture under an arch of roses. Then we had a cozy English dinner in the little cottage by the waterfalls. It was absolutely perfect!

I called home to talk to my family every night. I missed my kids! Some men would not have understood that, or would have gotten irritated, but Jerry said it was one of the reasons he had come to care for me so much and love me. He said he admired the importance I put on family and the love I have for them. He loved his own children and granddaughter very much, and he had a close relationship with his sisters and brother. They had lost their mother to cancer several years before. He knew the value of family.

When it was time to come home, Jerry drove the coastal route, stopping to see the giant redwoods along the way. It had been a wonderful vacation! I was so glad I saw it through to the end. What an adventure for me!

We weren't back long before we faced a new crisis, this time with Jerry. He was driving his Honda Prelude behind a large flatbed truck. The trucker unexpectedly hit his brakes hard and started to skid. Jerry hit his brakes, too, but there wasn't enough time to avoid an accident. The front of his car slid right under the bed of the truck. He was lucky he wasn't killed on impact! Sliding under the truck probably saved his life. Whew! That was a close one! I wasn't ready to be left alone again.

Jerry's new position meant fourteen-hour work days for him. I was working a 9 to 5 job. It seemed it might be a bit more difficult to get to know each other than we thought, but, on the other hand, he would be coming home to me each night, so we would have as much time together as we could. We managed to live an active social life with friends in both San Jose and Concord. We hosted parties, went to other people's homes, attended concerts and company parties, and bowled in a league. Jerry's daughter Lynn took line dance classes with us at the Saddle Rack in San Jose, and we took ballroom dancing with friends in Milpitas. I loved all the dancing!

There were a few things for Jerry to experience about my lifestyle. All my dairy items, meat, vegetables, bread, and Jewel T groceries were delivered to my house by Mr. King the delivery man. He was a very likeable person who was always very kind to me and the kids. One night as we were sleeping, Jerry heard a noise coming from the kitchen and asked if one of the kids was up. "No, that's the milkman," I replied. "Go back to sleep."

Jerry said, "What? You have a milkman? And he delivers at this time of night?" Apparently I hadn't told him about this before. We got up so he could meet Mr. King. On the way to the kitchen, I told Jerry, "I'm the last delivery on his route. He can only get here between 10:00 PM and midnight, so I leave the back door unlocked for him and he brings the groceries in. If I'm not up, he even puts them away for me. He leaves the bill on the kitchen table."

Naturally, Jerry was surprised that I would trust a delivery man so much that I would leave the house unlocked for him. With an incredulous expression on his face, he asked, "How do you know if he's left everything?"

I told him I'd met Mr. King through his daughter when she and I were attending beauty college together, so I felt I knew him and trusted him. Letting him enter my house unattended was never an issue with me.

We went to the kitchen and there was Alyssa, talking to the milkman. Their two complexions were so similar that Jerry was prompted to kiddingly say, "That must be the milkman's daughter."

I wasn't totally sure he was kidding, so I smiled and said, "No. She looks like me."

Mr. King delivered groceries to our house for one more year before he retired. By about 1982 it was no longer common to get home deliveries and I had to do the shopping in stores, just as Jerry did, and bring it all home in the station wagon. It was a big chore because I had to go to several different stores to get the best buys, and I couldn't leave the kids at home. All five children had to come with me. I used two shopping carts, pushing one, pulling the other. Two kids held onto my shirt so I could feel they were there, and two stood on the front end of each cart holding on. I always had Dale, Mr. Rambunctious, sit in the front cart where I could see him so there would be less chance of him running off.

I had some new things to learn about Jerry and his lifestyle, too. He worked for the Chevron oil company, and had been quickly promoted from truck driver to Lead Dispatcher in charge of the southeastern portion of the United States. At one of the company's summer barbecues, I had the opportunity to meet some of the other dispatchers and their families. After eating, we went into the community center to listen to music and dance. A man came up and asked if he could dance with me. Jerry said it was okay, so I went onto the dance floor with him. He said, "You must feel like you've got quite a catch with Jerry, being as you're a Mexican and a single mother with five kids. You must really think you've come up in the world with him." I found his comment offensive, but it was the tone of his voice and his attitude that I really disliked.

I looked at him and coolly said, "I don't need anybody judging me, least of all a bigot like you!" I didn't really know what the word bigot meant, and I'd never used it before, but I quickly decided he was one. He looked at me a little stunned. I told him the dance was over and walked away. I told Jerry what had been said. At first he didn't want to believe that someone would say something so prejudiced. I was a little hurt that Jerry didn't go back to say something, to defend me. It was many years later that I began to understand that because he had never encountered bigotry before, he probably didn't know quite how to handle the situation. In addition, he may have thought it wasn't worth the time to confront him. The comments would have no lasting impact on our lives, and we would not likely be seeing him again, so why bother. It was easier to ignore it, not to stress about it, and to move on. As the saying goes, "Consider the source." Fortunately, there were other, more pleasant people at the picnic, and I was soon distracted talking to them.

One of the women employees, Jan, was dating one of the other dispatchers who was one level above Jerry on the corporate ladder. She and I began talking about ourselves and realized we had a lot in common. We found that in the corporate world, the wife or girlfriend of an employee at the middle management level was expected to act prim and proper. I felt I had to look and behave a certain way. My clothing style changed drastically, and I had my hair done at a salon. I was very protective of my past. I wanted to be careful so that no one could criticize either of us. I felt I had to be on guard all the time. I didn't want to do anything that might possibly embarrass Jerry.

The one salvation to all this was one of the other wives. At all the company Christmas parties, Sara would eagerly look for me. She wasn't particularly subtle about it. When she saw us arrive, she'd yell, "Anita, come sit by me!" I liked her because I felt I could be myself with her. We weren't phony with each other, and we had a fun relationship. We both liked doing crafts and being creative, so we talked a lot about anything and everything to do with crafts.

One morning in July, my employers at the feed supply store where I had worked for about eight months, came to my house. I invited them in, not knowing why they were there. At first they were reluctant to come in, but I said, "Please, come in. I'm right in the middle of feeding my kids breakfast." It turned out they were there to fire me. They explained it was because I often arrived ten minutes late for work. They hadn't believed me when I told them that I was late because I had to wait for my mother's caregiver to arrive. They assumed it was an excuse I made up to cover for being out every night and unable to wake up early enough the next day to get to work on time. Just as they were handing me my last check, Mom rolled into the room in her wheelchair. I watched them look at her and become visibly uncomfortable. With unplanned, but perfect, timing, Rose arrived, late as usual. She said, "Anita, I'm sorry. I know I'm always late."

The people from the feed store said they were sorry, but they did have to let me go. I think their family secretly wanted me to leave because their son was not happy that I kept refusing his advances.

While at the time losing my job caused a lot of stress, it actually gave me more time to be with my mother, my kids, Rocky, and Jerry over the next six months. I could take care of Mom and get to know Jerry better.

This was an unexpected challenge for all of us. With Jerry living with us, it gave him a chance to learn first-hand about my family in all its glory. He was very supportive and helped out where he could, helping the kids with their homework nearly every night, and even going to the parent teacher conferences at school. We wanted to check with the teachers to see if the way things were at home was affecting their school work or behavior.

When I decided to remodel the kitchen and entryway in my parents' Victorian home, Jerry was there, ready to help. We couldn't get any contractors to remove the lead paint from the redwood siding outside by sandblasting or power washing, so Jerry hand-sanded the whole exterior of the house. What a guy!

My mother was soon bedridden and needed to be turned every two hours to avoid bed sores. We gave her all the medications that her doctors prescribed for her. Her meals were prepared according to a healthy regimen for diabetics, which involved weighing all her food and keeping close track of the protein-carb balance. Her kidney functions were diminishing, and that, combined with the hardening of her arteries, caused confused thinking at times. Sometimes she thought I was her mother. It was difficult for me to see her confusion. Despite all that we tried to do for her at home, her condition worsened. In early November, she had another heart attack and was hospitalized. The doctors thought her care was too much for Rose and me alone to manage, so strongly suggested that she be placed in a care facility. This was a relief for me because I was concerned that if something else happened with her condition at home, I would not have ways to help her. The care facility would be able to address changes in her condition more rapidly, and, hopefully, keep her comfortable. The facility was clean and I was pleased with Mom's care there. The staff even arranged for us to have holiday meals with her.

I took the kids to see her sometimes, but didn't want them to be in a facility environment too much. One never knows what they might see in a skilled nursing home, and they were still children. I wanted them to keep happier memories of times spent with Mom when she was feeling better and acting more like the person they knew as Grandma.

On Christmas Eve, the doctors allowed Jerry and me to take Mom for a drive in the neighborhood so that she could see all the festive lights on people's homes and in their yards. She really enjoyed the outing and seeing all the decorations. It was so good to see her smile and act happy again. We returned Mom to her room at the facility about 6:00 PM and went home to open gifts with the kids. Christmas went well.

Jerry and I planned a New Year's Eve party for our families and close friends, some of whom also had children. It was going to be a fun family party. Later in the evening, Mom started calling me on the phone every five minutes, saying "they" were trying to kill her and to come get her. She couldn't tell me who "they" were. I knew the caregivers were taking good care of her and would not try to harm her. I also knew that sometimes people on certain medications become paranoid and easily frightened. I tried to reassure her that everything would be okay and told her I would be there in a while. I dressed up because I knew she always liked to see me gussied up. Before Jerry and I got out the door, though, the nursing home called. They said she had suffered another heart attack and to wait a little while before coming in. I had planned to see her shortly after midnight to greet her in the new year with the hope that she might do better. At 11:40 PM, the phone rang again, but this time it was her doctor calling to tell me the heart attack had been massive. She had died.

Just a year before, I had asked God to please help me care for her and to give us more time together. I wanted her to experience a few more happy moments during her final months. When I got the call that she had passed, I thanked God for allowing me to have that additional time with her. I had done everything I could to keep her comfortable and happy. We had no unfinished business between us, and I had no regrets. I would miss her, but, I knew that it was her time to leave me and go home to Him.

The funeral was delayed several days due to Mom's death occurring on a holiday. I was fine during this time, at peace because I knew Mom was in a better place. Connie had not stayed in touch with Mom for a few months. No one else in the family had come to help care for Mom or see her, but now they tried to come tell me what to do for the funeral. Connie came to the house asking what the arrangements were, but never discussed the expense or offered to help pay for anything. The funeral home was kind enough to allow me to set up a payment plan. Mom had more bills than assets, and I didn't have enough money at the time to cover the expenses. With all the medical bills from the last couple of years, the cost of the funeral, and estate taxes, I had to get a second mortgage on her house. The estate lawyer helped me get a loan at the rate of 24% interest. I had no choice but to take it.

Connie asked me why I wasn't more upset and distraught at losing Mom. Besides talking to God and getting support there, I was on auto-pilot. There were things that needed doing, and I seemed to be the only one willing to do them. Jerry mentioned that he and I had tickets to a concert. It had been his Christmas gift to me. I didn't see any reason not to go, and knew Mom would want us to attend, even under the circumstances. She always wanted me to be happy and enjoy life. Connie didn't see it that way and slapped me in the face, saying "Why aren't you crying and sad that your mother has passed away? She took care of you and you seem ungrateful. You were just here for a free place to live!"

"Who are you to say *I'm* ungrateful? I didn't see *you* come to take care of her or even visit her. I was here to help her and Rocky, not to get any benefits for me! Besides that, I don't see anyone else offering to help take care of Rocky now that Mom is gone. Mom would want Jerry and me to go to the concert, and we're going no matter what you or anyone else thinks!" Connie and her family left the house saying they would see us at the funeral.

A short time after that, there was a knock at the door. I could see through the window that it was my ex-husband Jack, whom I hadn't seen for almost a year. I panicked, running to Jerry, saying, "Jack is here. He's here! What do you think he wants?" I didn't know if I should answer the door.

Jerry didn't know what to do either. All he could think about was what I had told him about the time Jack shot at me and I barely escaped. Jerry said he'd go with me to answer the door. Cautiously, I opened the door and asked in a neutral voice, "What are you doing here?"

Quietly, Jack said, "I came to tell you how sorry I am about your mother. She was a very good person. My brothers and I, along with a few friends, would like to play our Mariachi music and sing at her funeral, if you'll let us. We want to do this in her memory."

I was stunned. It seemed to be a nice gesture, and Mom always enjoyed their music, so I gave my permission for the band to play at the funeral. The afternoon of the funeral, we all arrived at the cemetery and gathered around the gravesite where the priest said a few words. Jack and his band played several of Mom's favorite songs. It was a solemn service. The music brought out even more emotion as we all remembered Mom and the things she liked and did. After they lowered her casket next to Dad's grave, we left. Everyone came to the house, ate, and shared more memories of Mom and the life she led. By the time people left, I was exhausted. I was ready for things to quiet down.

Little did I know what lay ahead!

Miss you, Mom

14. Life Goes On

It was 1982, the beginning of a new year. We continued to live in the home Mom and Dad left for me in San Jose. With Mom and Dad both gone now, Rocky's total care was in my hands. I needed to meet with his social worker to find out how to get legal guardianship of Rocky. Without that documentation, he would be moved into a group care home. He really didn't want that, nor did I. They knew I was already caring for him and that he was in a safe place, so for the time being they granted me Temporary Conservatorship.

After Mom had moved to the skilled nursing facility and was recovering well, it seemed like a reasonable time to take on a job. I wanted to contribute to the household income. Selling Avon products looked like a good fit for me because it would allow me the flexibility in schedule I needed. I could still care for my kids and Rocky, see Mom every day, and keep things going at home. After her death, that same flexibility gave me the time to take care of settling her estate. In a fairly short period of time, I had managed to sell $7,200 in Avon products, which put me into sales leadership status. I had no idea that I could be that good as a sales person! Avon put me in charge of sixty-seven territories and the supervision of thirty sales representatives. I continued selling to customers one on one as well. Going door to door was not easy for me, though. One time I was greeted by a naked man at the door who asked me to come in. Needless to say, I politely said "No, thank you," and left as quickly as I could! It left me feeling leery about selling door to door, at least in that neighborhood.

When I rang the doorbell at another house in the same neighborhood, I was greeted by a man carrying a rifle. He was holding back a Doberman Pincer who was barking and snarling at me. I nervously said, "I'm sorry. I guess the lady of the house isn't in," and quickly walked back to the sidewalk. After those experiences, I realized the job could potentially be dangerous and I wanted to find another job.

Fortunately, my friend Megan, who was a manager at Montgomery Wards, hired me for a position there. At first I worked in the dressing rooms, then worked my way up to doing store displays, which I *really* enjoyed. It allowed me to be creative, and I gained experience with merchandising products. Little did I know this would get me started on a lifelong career path in marketing and sales!

In the meantime....wouldn't you know it, Jack's issues came back to haunt me. Because I was still getting medical coverage for the kids through the county, I was required to report any and all earnings. Now that I had a job and income, the welfare department sent me a letter saying that Jack needed alimony. They also expected me to pay them back for the General Assistance money he had been collecting for several months. He was also trying to claim Mom's house was community property. Now that she was gone, he wanted half of the house. Fortunately, since her death occurred *after* our divorce, he was not entitled to any part of the house.

Soon after receiving that letter, another one arrived, this time from the state of Arizona. Jack's daughter Penelope had just had a baby in Arizona. They now expected me to pay for the expenses associated with the recent birth! I was upset. Why should I pay for his expenses, much less his daughter's?

I wrote to the California Welfare Department, explaining that I had documentation to prove that Jack and I had been divorced for over a year. His expenses and reimbursement to the General Assistance Program were HIS responsibility, not mine. As for alimony, he was not paying any child support to me and I had full responsibility for the kids, so I felt he was not entitled to any money at all from me.

I also responded to the letter from Arizona, telling them I did not feel obligated to pay for *his* daughter's expenses because I am *not* her birth mother, and her father and I were divorced before the baby was even conceived. The letters must have done the trick, as I received no further notices from the Welfare Departments of California or Arizona. Thank goodness those issues were taken care of, but I knew that in the future I would still have to deal with the fact that the judge had granted Jack visitation rights to see Dale and Alyssa. I was strongly opposed to them being exposed to his lifestyle, but I knew it would take some time to get the judge to revise the visitation rights.

I continued working at Wards for the next twelve months. I was in charge of supervising employees in five departments, as well as ordering merchandise. When the company decided to make Megan's position obsolete, they expected me to take over her job. That upset me. They were not only going to get rid of the person who had graciously hired me, but they were not offering me enough pay for all the work I was doing. I refused their offer. I applied for, and got, a job with JC Penney's as Assistant Manager in the Men's Department. It looked like a career path in sales was working well for me.

My love life was blossoming, too! Jerry loved me, and I had fallen in love with him. He truly cared for me, and respected me as only Paul had so many years before. Jerry was a good, kind, stable person. I really felt I could truly trust him. (I know, I say "truly" a lot. But I truly mean what I say!)

We started to discuss marriage, but we decided to wait for my kids to adjust to the idea before we got too involved in planning the wedding.

One evening in 1984, we were sitting talking about how quickly the last three years of living together had passed. The kids came into the room. The three older ones said they wanted to talk to us. Almost in total unison, they said that it was okay with them if we got married! We were a bit surprised at the way they announced their feelings, but we were happy to have their approval and blessings. Now we could really get started with planning our future together! We were happy and excited.

Thinking about my future.

15. Wedding Bells

"This day I will marry my friend,
The one I laugh with, live for, dream with, love."[2]

Each year, Jerry plans the Ford family reunion. The event lasts for a week during the summer, and usually takes place at a different location each year. We decided that the reunion that year would be a good time for us to be married. Nearly everyone in his family would be there, and my family could join us. It felt like the perfect plan.

After considering several wedding sites, we decided to get married at the Ponderosa Ranch at Incline Village in Lake Tahoe, California. The fun part was that it had been the set of a popular 1960's TV show when we were kids: "Bonanza." Nearby Tahoe City had a lot to offer families in the way of accommodations and activities. The ranch had a small, white, prairie chapel, complete with a quaint-looking steeple. It was built in the late 1800's and would be a lovely site for the exchange of our wedding vows.

The day of the wedding, while driving to the chapel, it occurred to me that Jerry had never officially asked me for my hand in marriage. When I commented on that, he asked, "Are you sure I didn't?"

"No, you never did."

He pulled the car over to the side of the road and proposed to me right there in the car. Of course, I said "YES! After all the plans we've made and with people arriving, would you expect me to say anything else?"

"Well, you could say no," he said. We both had a good

---

[2] Author unknown. Quote from Anita and Jerry's wedding invitation (1984).

laugh and I reassured him I did want to marry him. Jerry smiled and said, "We'd better get going, or we'll be late for our own wedding!" I love Jerry's sense of humor as well as his romantic side.

Everyone was waiting for us at the chapel. I wore an ankle-length, cream-colored Victorian dress that seemed fitting for the vintage atmosphere at the Ponderosa. Jerry wore a camel-colored suit with a pink and cream striped tie that coordinated with my dress and flowers. We made quite a good-looking bride and groom, if I do say so myself.

Just before the ceremony was to begin, I sat in the Bride's Room suddenly feeling a bit uncertain, questioning if I should be marrying again. Would this be another mistake? Would Jerry's family, especially his kids, accept me as his wife? I told myself, 'You know you love him. You know you want to be with him.' But, there was a lingering question: Would I regret it later?

The processional music began to play. It was time for me to enter the chapel. The preacher, who was also the town sheriff and saloon bartender, looked for me. I didn't appear. Jerry and his father, the Best Man, were at the altar. The wedding march started several times, and the one hundred or so seated guests began to get antsy.

I was still in the Bride's room, nervously pondering. Jerry's daughter Lynn came to me with something blue to put in the purse that I was going to carry down the aisle. She reminded me of the saying, *Something old, something new, something borrowed, something blue.* She said the blue token was for good luck. That simple gesture helped me to feel more comfortable that I might be accepted as her father's wife, and it really was okay to be getting married again. I felt this wedding would be my last.

Reassured that I was doing the right thing, I left the Bride's

Room and walked to the front entrance of the chapel where sixteen-year-old Linda and fourteen-year-old Miguel were waiting for me. The delay was really only about fifteen minutes, but at the time it felt like an eternity to me as well as probably to the guests who were there to witness our marriage ceremony.

Linda walked in front of me as my Maid of Honor. Miguel walked me down the aisle, and as we approached the altar he put my hand in Jerry's. As part of the ceremony, the preacher asked, "Do we have anyone here who objects to this marriage?" Jerry knew his father was the type to raise his hand as a joke, so he turned to him and put his index finger to his lips, indicating he should remain silent. He loudly shushed him as well, which was heard by all in the chapel and got everyone rolling with laughter.

Although I was so nervous that Jerry could hardly hear me say my vows, the ceremony proceeded without further delays or complications. We at last vowed to be husband and wife. This was truly the wedding and husband of my dreams. I had met a man who loved me for me, and whom I loved. His daughter, son, and granddaughter were wonderful, and I wanted to be part of that family, too. All that, plus he liked my kids and they liked him! It felt perfect!

After the wedding, with Jerry wearing a vintage-style top hat, we posed for photos. Shortly after that, a classic 1948 Chrysler Limousine drove us down the hill to our car. Family members had decorated the car with the traditional "Just Married," and tin cans trailed behind the back bumper. It was a fun ride to the reception at a large chalet in Tahoe City.

We had rented the three-story chalet for both the wedding reception and the Ford family reunion. I loved that I could toss my bridal bouquet from the third floor. People were allowed to pitch their tents on the grounds surrounding the house. It worked out quite well for both events.

We were very fortunate that Eloise, whom Jerry knew from his childhood days, was experienced in planning social events. She did a wonderful job coordinating the reception so that I didn't have to do a thing, and the timing went smoothly. Everything from when to cut the cake and to throwing the bouquet was perfect!

The reception was so much fun! The thought of the delay due to my second thoughts now made us laugh. Jerry, in his typical humorous way, said he had been waiting so long he thought I had skipped town! And we had to chuckle again at Jerry's loud shushing of his father. All in all, it was a beautiful, memorable day!

One of the things that made our wedding event different for Jerry's family was that he was the first to marry outside of their ethnic culture. Our guests were people from all walks of life and a variety of cultural backgrounds. There were Chevron truckers and their families, an American Indian, an interracial couple (which was not common then), and one person who drove up in their family car a hearse! Another guest, Bob, was a member of the Hell's Angels. He and Jerry had become friends at Chevron where they both worked. To this day, we have the gift Bob and his date Rosemary gave us: two motorcycle postage stamps in a picture frame. Written on the back of the frame is "Too good to be forgotten." We haven't forgotten them either.

Miguel and Jerry's granddaughter gave us a fun gift in the form of a talent show. Miguel did break-dancing. Brandy, a preschooler, sang and danced to the tunes of the "Itsy Bitsy Spider" and "Little White Duck." Everyone loved the show!

We were exhausted by the end of the evening, and looking forward to beginning our honeymoon. However, it was not in the cards to start out as your typical honeymoon. Two days before the wedding, Jerry's brother, Al, and his family were driving up from Long Beach when their car broke down in Bridgeport. They were able to hitch a ride in a pickup truck to Carson City, Nevada, but they had to sit in the bed of the truck. Wouldn't you know, there was a rainstorm that day? They were drenched by the time they got to Carson City! They sure were troopers! We were glad they could make it to the wedding, so we didn't mind delaying the start of our honeymoon and drove them back to Bridgeport the day after the wedding to get their car from the repair shop.

Most family members stayed at the chalet for the rest of the reunion. Jerry and I left the kids under their care so that we could go to the Hilton Hotel in Reno, Nevada, for a romantic honeymoon night. As luck would have it, the air conditioning broke down at the hotel after a fire in the building earlier that day. No rooms would be available until later that night. It was mid-August and *very* hot! While the Hilton was trying to fix their air conditioning, we spent five to six hours going in and out of different casinos that did have working air conditioners. Finally, at 2:00 AM, we could comfortably go to our reserved room. We were so tired, but happy that we were married at last.

Part of the planned reunion activities included a side trip to the ghost town called Bodie. The kids wondered if they would see any ghosts while they were there wandering around the town.

Two days later we attended a Sports Car Olympics Race at Boreal Ridge that was sponsored by the Northern California Sports Car Council. We participated in all ten competitions with our Prelude. Several events were time and distance rallies with check points. The routes took us on streets in nearby cities. All participating vehicles were supposed to maintain a speed of sixty MPH. The front seat passenger was the navigator.

The Funkhana race was in the Boreal Ridge parking lot. Participants had to do challenges along the course. At one station, we had to both get out of the car and I had to push Jerry around it while he was sitting on a mechanic's cart. Try doing that in high heels!

I had never competed in any type of race before, and I was thrilled that we won several trophies. We placed in the Top Ten out of three hundred entries! What a different, but fun, type of honeymoon!

It had been a bit of work with all the preparations to organize the wedding *and* reunion, but it was all worth it. It was a great start to our new life together as husband and wife.

16. Jerry and Chevron

After the wedding, we went back to our usual work routine. Jerry was doing very well in his job at Chevron, and soon earned another promotion, this time in a position at the corporate headquarters in San Francisco. He was now part of the Executive Staff. He had to divide his time between managing the company garages as fleet administrator and coordinating the motor pools and thirteen corporate chauffeurs. In addition, he was to tend to the various requests from the executives. There was so much to learn, there was a thirty-day training period.

Security and privacy were essential aspects of the new position. Jerry knew how to be confidential. He went by the old-fashioned adage that "Loose lips sink ships." His efficiency, attitude, and ability to maintain a sense of privacy kept him in everyone's favor.

This position required that Jerry be on site at 6:30 AM. His office phone would start ringing soon after his arrival, and he stayed as late as required. The word "No" was not in his vocabulary. It was that attitude that made him an asset to those at the top, and kept everything running smoothly. Need a car brought to you at Lake Tahoe? "Sure thing…" Need 40 tickets to see the musical Beach Blanket Babylon for a specific date, and on short notice? "Not a problem." Want permission from PG & E and the city to park a tanker truck on the sidewalk on Market Street in downtown San Francisco? "I'll have it for you tomorrow." There was always something different. He never knew what the day would bring. Sometimes requests required more personal attention for the top execs in the company. On occasion Jerry was asked to buy shoes or give up his tie to an executive who got dressed in the dark and hadn't coordinated his accessories.

One day Jerry received a phone call from Jimmy Stewart, asking if someone could pick him up at the Burlingame Country Club. Politely, Jerry responded, "Yes, can you hold a minute, please?" Thinking this was a joke, Jerry put a hand over the receiver and asked one of the chauffeurs, "Who would call and do a poor imitation of Jimmy Stewart?" The chauffeurs told him that it really *was* the actor Jimmy Stewart! He was related by marriage to a former CEO and came every Thanksgiving to be with family.

Another time, a tea was planned. The morning of the tea, he was asked to get eleven autographed copies of a book written by George P. Schultz, the former Secretary of State in the Reagan administration. He was on Chevron's Board of Directors at the time. It was already 9:00 AM, and Jerry had to have the books by 1:00 PM. Talk about short notice! Jerry's answer to the request was, "Let me see what I can do." He wasn't certain he was going to be able to do it, but he sure was going to try. Mr. Schultz had an office at Stanford University. Jerry called Schultz's secretary and asked, "If I bring eleven books over for Mr. Schultz to sign, do you think he could write a little note in each one?"

The secretary said she would see what she could arrange. He hurried over to Stanford. Schultz graciously autographed all of the books, and Jerry made it back to SF in time for the tea. Nothing seemed impossible for this dedicated employee!

Part of Jerry's corporate position included being part of Chevron's Security Team. As a consequence, he was in contact with many notable people, including Eldridge Cleaver and Condoleezza Rice. He met movie star Cliff Robertson. Later, he met Carol Channing when she did a red, white, and blue 'Hello, Dolly' promotion for the company.

At the time, half the executive board members were not Chevron employees. The list of outside directors ran the gamut of

CEO's of companies such as Bechtel, Bank of America, Ralston Purina, Chrysler, Peterbilt, Hewlett-Packard, and others. One member was a former White House cabinet member and politician. Jerry responded to requests from all of them.

Another part of his job description included taking care of the marketing department's needs, which meant taking the lead on organizing various company lunches. As a result, Jerry had two offices; one in San Ramon, the other in San Francisco. The company did not give him a budget, which at times made things difficult or awkward. There were no company credit cards then, and Jerry was expected to pay cash for everything and be reimbursed later. Sometimes that meant shuffling our personal funds to pay for things until the reimbursement arrived.

On the home front, our personal relationship was one of mutual respect. I realized I was "the boss' wife." I wanted to support him in his career, so I encouraged him and admired his accomplishments.

There is an old saying: "Behind every great man, there is a great woman," and that is how Jerry saw me in his life. He credited part of his advancements and success to me.

In return, he encouraged me to follow my dreams and explore whatever new career ventures I wanted to pursue. We worked well together.

We are a winning team!

17. New Jobs, New Home, New Challenges

Before our wedding I was working for JC Penney's. Unfortunately, the job was not very challenging and I had become uncomfortable with the work environment. One particular male customer came to my department on a daily basis, trying to pursue a relationship with me. I informed him I was not interested and was engaged to be married, but he continued to come every day nevertheless. He would ask me questions about how garments should fit. It was an uncomfortable situation for me. On top of that, I was used to multi-tasking and keeping busy every minute. This position was too mundane for me. I was standing around a lot of the time with little to do.

I wanted a new job that would be more challenging and rewarding for me, plus have better pay. Jerry and I often went to a restaurant in a local strip mall in San Jose. One night as we passed by the store window of Fry's Supermarket, I noticed a Help Wanted sign. I remember going into the store, filling out the application, and getting an immediate interview. During the interview with the Assistant Store Manager, I told him, "Here's the deal. I don't push shopping carts or bag or carry groceries. And I do *not* clean bathrooms or mop floors. I *do* bring retail management skills, as well as experience in marketing and customer service. I will be dedicated and give you one hundred ten percent of me. I can do almost anything you are willing to train me to do. Take it or leave it."

With a look of surprise on his face, the manager responded, "You're assertive enough to get your point across. I'll let you know in a couple of days."

It was my turn to be surprised the next day when he called and said, "We'd like you work for us as our new General

Merchandise Assistant." I was extremely excited. The way I had spoken during the interview, I assumed I had been too assertive. I didn't expect to be hired. I accepted the offer, with the contingency that I start with them after giving my current employer two weeks' notice. It seemed only fair that Penney's have the opportunity and time to find and train my replacement. I would show my new employer that same courtesy should I leave them some day. I think he appreciated my candor and the courtesy to my employers. He went along with the contingency. When I gave my notice, I told Penney's I was quitting for personal reasons, and two weeks later I started my new job at Fry's.

With Jerry's promotion to Chevron's Executive Staff, he was required to live within a forty-five to sixty-minute drive to his office in San Francisco. Our location in San Jose at the time was too far away. We needed to move. Since we didn't want to sell our rental homes that we were keeping for extra income, we had to find the down payment money elsewhere. Jerry sold his prized collectible 1968 root beer-colored Corvette to get the money. I appreciated his sacrifice.

It was a seller's market. Competition for homes was keen. After several weeks of looking at homes and being out-bid by other buyers, our bid on a house in Fremont was accepted. The location was reasonably close to BART, so Jerry would have the option of taking BART to San Francisco, or he could drive to the office in thirty to forty minutes. It doubled my commute from thirty minutes to an hour, but the distance was more of a requirement for Jerry's job than mine. We did what was necessary. This new house would be one that we could truly own jointly.

While we had been house hunting, one of our daughters, a young, inexperienced teenager, got involved with an older man. He seemed to have quite an influence on her. I didn't feel comfortable around him for some reason and didn't have a good feeling about the situation. We were worried about her and wanted to protect her. We went so far as to send her to live with relatives a distance away, hoping the separation would end the relationship. She soon ended up back home again, however, and they were still together. Before long, she was pregnant with his child. Jerry and I were paying for her medical insurance. She was eight months along when we were getting ready to move. Her doctor was in the San Jose area, so we allowed her to move in with her boyfriend so she would be close to the hospital when she went into labor.

We were trying to get settled into our new digs. The house itself suited our needs, having enough rooms for all of our family, plus one of Alyssa's girlfriends who needed a place to stay for a while. It was crowded, but all doable, and we were enjoying the new home. I wasn't crazy about the way the house was decorated. Jerry wouldn't let me start renovations like I had done at the San Jose house where I had knocked down walls, put up sheetrock, painted, and put up wall paper. Since I was working full-time, it would take a long while to complete that type of make-over. Understandably, he didn't want to come home to that kind of mess each night. I couldn't blame him after all the work of moving. We ended up living in the house for over twenty years with the same green and yellow color scheme as when we moved in! Each of the rooms had a different color carpet, too. It really didn't matter what the house looked like, though. It was *ours together*!

Our move to this nice, peaceful residential area of Fremont felt too quiet and "boring" for Linda, Miguel, Alyssa, and Dale, all active teens or preteens. At our previous home in San Jose something had *always* been happening in the neighborhood. Based on observations of different activities and behaviors, there were suspicions that the house next door was one of ill repute, and the one across the street appeared to be a drug house. Some of the neighbors conducted what appeared to be "shady dealings." The sound of police sirens was not an uncommon occurrence. It was a tough neighborhood.

In contrast, Fremont at that time was more like a suburb and there was a lot less activity. When we moved there, it was quite an adjustment for all of us. Jerry fit in well enough, but the Mexican-American heritage the kids and I share made us stand out in this community of mostly Caucasians. We overheard one neighbor say, "I guess there goes the neighborhood. We've got wetbacks moving in." That set the stage for me and my children. We felt we were not wanted in the neighborhood. Whether it was the cultural difference or some other reason, we were not accepted into the local Catholic church. They told us there was "no availability at this time." They suggested that another church might fit our needs better. I was very surprised. What church tells a person there is no room for them?

After our daughter gave birth to her son Don, we brought them to stay with us temporarily. She had no experience with infants or children and was not really prepared to be a mother, especially at the tender age of sixteen. We wanted to help her with the baby. After a few months, we asked her if she still wanted to marry this fellow. She said yes, she wanted to be with him. Jerry and I agreed to give permission for them to marry. We feared if we didn't, he could take her away, and we might not see her or our grandchild again.

A couple of months after their Reno wedding, I let them move into the house I had inherited from Mom and Dad. I did not expect rent from them and I paid most of their household bills. I took food and other household necessities over on a regular basis. It was very hard on me financially, but I wanted to provide what I could and help take care of our grandchild. Instinct told me the relationship with her partner was potentially dangerous for her. I knew from my own experience that all I could do was watch and be there for her if she needed me. It seemed to me that she was following in my footsteps by getting involved in what might potentially be an abusive relationship.

I never intended to pass the legacy of abuse on to my children. Observing what has happened to some of my children in their first relationships, I see that sometimes children who grow up seeing parents in abusive relationships may find themselves in similar situations as they meet new people. Often, they don't even know how they got there, just as I hadn't.

Author and motivational speaker Jon Acuff wrote, "Sometimes God redeems your story by surrounding you with people who need to hear your past, so it doesn't become their future."[3]

It is my hope that someone will read my story and learn from my experiences. I hope they can gain the courage they need to get away from abusive people in their life. It is essential for their own personal safety, but also for the sake of their children and their children's future. Try to break the cycle.

It wasn't long before our daughter was expecting another child. One day she called me saying she was hurting and didn't know what to do. I could tell by her voice that she was panicking. I wasted no time getting there. I almost literally flew! I made the thirty minute drive in fifteen minutes. When I arrived, I could see that her water had broken and she was in labor. I needed to take

---

[3] Many thanks to Jon Acuff at *acuff.me* for granting permission to use his quotation.

her to the hospital. We left Don with a neighbor and headed out the door. The ride would take forty-five minutes, and the contractions were coming faster and faster. I stopped the car and flagged down a policeman to see if he could give us a police escort. He initially said it was out of his jurisdiction, but he'd try to get authorization from his commander to take us anyway. He got the clearance to take us to the hospital. He was concerned the baby might arrive before we got there and told me I should ride in the backseat of the patrol car with her. That meant leaving my new Honda Prelude from Jerry behind. I hated that thought, but it was important I be with her right then. It was all pretty crazy!

The officer called ahead to the hospital to alert them he was bringing in a pregnant woman about to deliver. When we arrived, the staff took her right into the labor room. It wasn't long before they whisked her off to the delivery room. She was experiencing placenta previa, which means the placenta was separating from the baby's umbilical cord. The baby could die, and our daughter could hemorrhage to death. I was beside myself with worry. The officer who brought us to the hospital stayed with me for a bit to make sure I was going to be okay. He may have very well saved both of their lives by getting us there as quickly as he did. I will always be grateful for his kindness and consideration.

Two hours later, I had a new granddaughter! Tricia was put into an incubator in the Nursery. Her mother was very tired, but she was doing okay. I called Jerry to pick me up and, after some searching, we found my car again.

18. Life with Children

All of us were trying to adjust to the new surroundings. Jerry and I were beginning our new life as husband and wife with a solid relationship. We started out in the new house with my five active children. Jerry's daughter Lynn and her husband both worked for the Deputy Sheriff's office in San Jose. They were both required to work three and a half consecutive days each week, which meant many hours away from home and from their young daughter Brandy. Housing was so expensive in San Jose that they had moved outside the area to more affordable housing, but the trade-off was it greatly increased their commute time. Between the long work hours and the commute, Brandy's routine was often disrupted. Jerry and I said she could stay with us. We thought it might help them deal with the long hours. Were we up to the challenge of bringing another child into our brood? We thought we were.

Some days it felt like a three-ring circus! All of the kids were active and inquisitive. One of their larger adventures was when they made a 5-foot volcano in the driveway. They had taken the garden hose and propped it up while they piled gravel and dirt around it. When they turned the water on full force, it erupted violently, throwing the gravel and dirt everywhere. And I mean everywhere! It flew through open windows into the house, on top of the neighbor's prize roses, and onto the new siding of our freshly painted house. It was actually pretty creative on their parts, but I wasn't happy to see the mess when I arrived home after a long day at work. Kids!

It seemed like I ended up in the emergency room with one or the other of them every month. One time Linda had a serious cut just above one eye. Dale seemed to get injured the most, though. He was the most precocious of the bunch and got into more mischief. Emergency Room staff members soon learned to recognize me and just smile as I brought him in again. He slid down the stair banister that had a raised screw near the bottom that cut him from stem to stern. Another time he cut his cheek on broken glass. A third time he fell on a table and cut his chin wide open. There was never a dull moment!

As with many blended families, children either resent or are jealous of step-parents and have difficulty accepting the new situation. Our family was no different. Jerry's kids were older and living on their own, so their adjustment to me as their stepmom was quite different from my kids' adjustment to Jerry. For my kids, adjusting to having a new father figure in the house was a bit of a hurdle. They liked Jerry and had given their approval for us to get married, but we found that building healthy relationships between them was going to be challenging.

Dale was four years old when I got the divorce from his father Jack. He was too young to understand how Jack's actions had hurt me and his sisters. He had no recollection of the traumatic things that had happened and, in his mind, probably envisioned that we had a happy family life. He, like most children, had put his father on a pedestal. Consequently, he blamed Jerry for my break-up with Jack. This was far from the truth, if you recall my experiences with Jack, but Dale thought, and hoped, that one day his father and I would get back together. *I* knew that would never happen! When Jerry and I got married, Dale could see that Jerry was in my life to stay, and he wasn't too happy about it.

He gave Jerry a very hard time and he was relentless in his attempts to disrupt our lives. At times he became uncontrollable. If Jerry so much as opened a can of beer, he would become upset, telling Jerry, "Don't drink that, don't drink it!" We thought he was reacting to unconscious memories of seeing Jack's abusive behavior when he drank. Plus, it was something he could pester Jerry about.

I knew that Dale was intelligent. In fact, I sometimes felt he was too smart for his own good. At the age of five, he had taken apart electric can openers and was able to reassemble them so that they still worked. As he got older, one of our neighbors showed him how to take game cartridges apart and reprogram them, as well as how to create simple computer programs. He easily mastered anything electrical. The problem was that Dale was not focusing his energies and talents in the right direction. On one occasion, he rigged up the doorknob in the entryway so that when Jerry entered, it would give him an electric shock!

At age eleven, he was behaving like a rebellious fifteen-year-old. On the Fourth of July he made a rocket and it ended up going through one of our neighbor's windows. We had to replace not only the broken window, but the damaged carpet in their house. With the owners being county sheriffs, we were lucky those were the only consequences!

There were more instances where Dale tried to physically hurt Jerry. One day he balanced a rock over a doorway with the hope that it would hit Jerry on the head when he came through the door. Fortunately, the rock only hit Jerry's hand and he was okay. At that point, I was at my wit's end, not knowing how to handle these situations.

Later that year, believe it or not, Dale robbed a gas station. How many eleven-year-olds do you know who would do that? He was too young to be placed in Juvenile Hall, and the court offered no help. He was released into our custody. I was frustrated. I didn't want him to get away with it. I wanted him to find out that there would be consequences for his actions. As a consequence at home I tried taking away his electronic games and electrical components, things I thought meant a lot to him. He had so many things and so many hiding places for them that it didn't seem to matter to him. *Nothing* I did seemed to faze him.

Dale's behavior began to impact people outside the family, too. He stole from friends and altered checks that we had signed so that he could increase the amount on the check and get the additional money for himself. When he was caught and confronted about the thefts, he never showed any remorse. As a responsible parent wanting to raise responsible children, this was *very* frustrating and infuriating! How does one instill a sense of responsibility and ethics into such a rebellious person?

19. The Roller Coaster Continues

I continued working for Fry's Supermarket, which by now had been sold to Save Mart. I was learning a great deal about marketing and ordering merchandise, as well as managing employees. Originally I was hired as an assistant in the General Merchandise Department. Four months later, the manager of that department was promoted to Assistant Store Manager, so I was then promoted to General Merchandise Manager. In addition, I was responsible for managing the Liquor Department. When the Deli Department was short-handed, I stepped in to help them. My goal was to work for ten years in the supermarket industry, then retire from that line of work. I worked hard and was proud of the fact that this store maintained the status of being Number One in the franchise district for three years.

Both of the store managers knew I would give my all on the job. I had a good rapport with them and was allowed a considerable amount of flexibility with work hours. If I needed to take two hours off, I could let the Manager know, clock out, and return later to complete my hours for the day. If I needed a day or two off for personal reasons, that was allowed. I felt really good that my employers acknowledged that I was conscientious, reliable, honest, and would get things done. One time, a winery representative put their wine in space designated for another winery. I told them to take their wine and leave the store, pointing out that they were completely out of line. "Other companies pay for their spaces. I am certain they would not want anyone else's product on *their* shelf!" The manager who observed the incident was concerned that there could be backlash from the winery. Fortunately, the vendor returned with no further infractions on other vendors' spaces and with no complaints about me.

When Valentine's Day came around that year, Jerry surprised me at the store. He thought of everything, and even brought dressy clothes for me to change into after work. He escorted me out the door, holding an extra-large umbrella over my head to keep me from getting wet in the rain. The umbrella also obstructed my view. When we got to the curb, he slowly raised the umbrella and I saw an elegant-looking limousine. I felt like Cinderella! As Jerry opened the door for me, I saw our friend Squiggy in the driver's seat, looking so debonair in his black suit and chauffeur's hat. Reservations had been made at the Hilltop Country Club for a pre-ordered lobster dinner for two. Jerry planned the evening with attention to detail, wanting us to have an elegant dinner fit for royalty. Unfortunately, however, when I started to eat the lobster, I became squeamish and started to gag. I had never eaten lobster before, and I didn't like the texture or the flavor. I asked if I could have a steak instead, which, of course, was then served to me. Jerry never blinked an eye about my request for a different entrée. Little did I know at the time that he had prepaid for the lobster dinner and had to pay an even higher price for the additional steak! We had champagne and a decadent dessert which was so rich I couldn't eat it, so I asked for a scoop of chocolate ice cream instead. The evening was very romantic, like something out of a movie. I really loved all the special arrangements Jerry had made to make it such a beautiful evening.

Jerry has always been so good to me. He spoiled me again that year with a brand new metallic blue Honda Prelude as a Christmas gift. He took the time to creatively hide the key in the middle of our Christmas tree. I was so surprised!

At home that year, issues were still coming up with Dale. Linda kept reminding him how his father had mistreated her. I think Dale had mixed feelings about that. How could his father, whom he idolized, have behaved so inappropriately with his sister? At the same time, he may have felt protective of Linda, which led to a sense of guilt. Combine all that with raging teenage hormones and an unwanted stepfather in the house and you have a prescription for a troubled youth.

We went to court multiple times for his various offenses. It seemed to us that the judge always acted as if Dale's misbehavior was insignificant. One day I decided I'd had enough! Out of sheer desperation and extreme frustration, I forced him to get in the car. He was a teenager now and old enough to be placed in Juvenile Hall. I drove him there. I told the person in charge, "*Please* put my son in jail. Maybe if he spends some time here, he might find out he doesn't want to be in jail and will change his ways." They kept him over the weekend, at *our* expense, but, once again, the judge released him. This time at least they told us the whole family should go for counseling, and gave us a referral to a counselor.

The other children disliked the counseling sessions, and resented that they had to go because of Dale. Alyssa in particular felt she did not belong there and rebelled. When Jerry and I got married, Alyssa was eleven years old. She was especially close to me, and was not willing to share me with anyone else, nor did she like another adult telling her what to do. She thought *I* should be the one to decide all the rules for the family. All the kids had experienced so much over the years with men who did not stay in their lives. She, like the others, was probably leery that Jerry would be just another transitional person in her life. It all contributed to her feelings of not wanting to be involved in the counseling. She was one of the only ones who would speak up during the sessions, however, so the counselor called on her more than the others. She wasn't too happy about that, but the counselor needed to hear from the children in the family.

After a few appointments, the counselor suggested that since Dale wanted to be with his father, he should at least be allowed to spend weekends with him. I was concerned that Jack was still drinking too much and worried that he would not supervise Dale enough. Against my better judgement, I decided to let Dale have what he wanted – to be with his father on weekends.

Dale stayed with Jack, his live-in girlfriend, and their two children off and on for the next two years. He stayed with us in Fremont on school days, and spent weekends and most holidays at their house. We dropped Dale off at school, but we later learned that as soon as we were out of sight, he left the school grounds. After many unexcused absences, the high school called to say they were expelling him from the regular school and sending him into the district's continuation high school. Needless to say, we were surprised to hear of all the absences, much less his expulsion from school! Dale attended classes at the continuation school some of the time, but skipped out often. The continuation school called us into the office one day, asking if we knew why he was missing so much school. I told them that I had made arrangements with my employer to go in a bit later so I could walk him to the door each day, and that we were not aware until then that he was not staying in class. The counselor speculated that with that kind of behavior, drugs might be an issue. I left the school feeling bewildered. Jerry and I thought we were doing what we could to help him adjust to being a teenager in a new school with new friends and a new stepfather. How could he have a drug problem? I realized that maybe I couldn't see what Dale was going through emotionally.

Jack was no help with the situation. I tried to tell him what the counselor said, and strongly encouraged him to spend more time with Dale. I asked him to be more observant. It made no difference. As I had anticipated, Jack did not spend much time with Dale or oversee his behavior. In fact, Jack's girlfriend spent more time with Dale than Jack did. Dale wanted no part of that family any more than he wanted Jerry in his life. When at Jack's home, he seemed to focus on breaking up Jack's new relationship. When he succeeded at doing just that, Jack immediately sent Dale packing back to us. In one way, I was relieved. Maybe under our roof we could figure something out to help him. It would take some time, and a *whole lot* of patience. We hoped and prayed for wisdom to know how to help him get through this phase in his life, and also for a miracle that could turn Dale's life around for the better.

20. More Options

Miguel had been a bit of a problem as a teenager, too. Toward the end of his high school days, he started using our house as a hotel, bringing his girlfriend over while Jerry and I were at work. I did not approve of this, and I didn't want Alyssa and Dale to get the idea this kind of thing was allowed in our house or encouraged. I warned Miguel that if the visits did not stop, he could go live with his girlfriend at her house. He continued to bring her over. The day after he graduated high school, I was true to my word. I packed up his belongings and put them on the porch. He thought I was kidding. I didn't relent, and he ended up going to live with friends because the girlfriend's foster parents would not allow him to live in their home either.

We had so much going on in our lives at that point! There were Dale, Rocky, and our other children to supervise and care for, and both Jerry and I worked full time to make ends meet.

In 1989, Sophia, the friend who had introduced Jerry to me, bought a travel agency in San Jose with her partner Theodore. They served mostly the travel needs of corporations. They wanted to develop the leisure side of travel and add casual customers to their clientele. Previously, in the Spring of 1987, we had gone with them on a cruise to the Eastern Caribbean. I had never traveled outside the country before, so it was exciting for me, and I found out I liked travel! Although I knew nothing about being a travel agent, Sophia asked me to work for them to help expand their business. I was still working at Save Mart, but I could always use the extra money, and I like new experiences, so I said yes. I learned a lot through on-the-job training about how to find the best travel itineraries and made reservations on behalf of our clients.

Looking back, I don't quite know how I handled so much! Besides taking care of the family, I was working two jobs. In addition, my girlfriend Tina and I decided it would be great to have our own business, so we started up a limousine service. Jerry helped us buy two used limousines. One was a blue stretch limo, the other a formal white Cadillac. We bought candy apple red cumber bunds with matching ties, and white pleated dress shirts to wear with stylish black pants and jackets. We left hats for the gentlemen chauffeurs. We were hired for graduations, weddings, and wine trips, and provided service to and from theaters. Our customers heard about us through word of mouth, and we soon had a good client base with repeat customers. When I worked at the travel agency, we offered our limousine services to their customers as well. At times, we were so much in demand that we had to turn business away!

My favorite time was when a co-worker from Save Mart planned to take his date to the opera in San Francisco. He had me order appetizers, shrimp cocktails, champagne, and Godiva chocolates. It was a picnic in a limo! To add to our fun, as we dropped him off at his home at the end of the evening, he graciously gave us a seventy-five dollar tip!

The limousine business came to an end one weekend when the reality of the responsibility hit us. We were hired to take a small group of high school students to their prom. We picked the teens up at the designated home. As we were about to leave, the kids rolled down a back window and one of the parents handed them a bottle of what I presumed was sparkling cider. About a half mile away, I heard a pop and realized it was really a bottle of champagne. I was not willing to risk going to jail or losing my licenses by allowing minors to consume alcohol on my watch. I pulled to the side of the road and took the bottle away, saying "I'll be giving this back to your mother." To top things off, after the prom the kids asked me to take them to a hotel. Personally, it went against my better judgment. I did not lecture them, but did ask if their parents knew about their plans. They said yes, so I took them to the hotel, at which point they said they didn't need me anymore because they were spending the night there. I drove back to the home where I had picked the kids up and spoke with the parents about the arrangements. I was not happy with their answer that they were allowing the kids to stay overnight in the hotel. I refunded their money and made it quite clear that I was no longer responsible for whatever might happen after I left the kids at the hotel. That experience led me to believe that providing limousine service was not the business for me. I did not want to risk being put in *that* position again! After discussing the incident with my business partner, we decided to close the business and I sold the limos.

Meanwhile, back at the travel agency, things went very well for the few months I worked there. Then a new owner bought the agency. As a result of the booming technology in Silicon Valley, he wanted the company to go back to being strictly for corporate customers. He brought in his own team, all well-versed in technology, and let the old staff go. I liked the travel business, and found other employment for a short time with an agency in Sunnyvale. My experience as a travel agent has come in very handy for travel in other jobs and for our own personal trips.

21. Rock and Roll in '89

The proximity of our home to Jerry's San Francisco office turned out to be particularly important on October 17, 1989, when the Loma Prieta Earthquake hit the Bay Area. I remember that day vividly. Jerry was going to go with me to a travel seminar that night at the Sunset Magazine headquarters in Menlo Park. My instinct told me something was unusual that day. Something BIG was going to happen. That afternoon I paced the floor from the kitchen into the living room, back to the bedrooms, and through nearly every part of the house. I couldn't stop walking. I've learned over the years that when I start unconsciously pacing like that, something important is going to happen. I felt *very* uneasy and wanted Jerry to come home early from work because I was feeling anxious and didn't know why. I wanted him with me. I must have called him at least twenty times, repeating my request that he return home *before* 5:00 o'clock, which was the time he usually left the office.

Jerry heeded my request for an early departure from work. True to form with my previous experiences of feeling this kind of anxiety, something BIG did happen! The moment Jerry got home at 5:04 PM, the earthquake hit! They say it lasted fifteen seconds, but it sure felt longer than that! We heard on the news that a BART train that left shortly after Jerry did was stopped in the tunnel. BART employees guided passengers from the train cars into the tunnel and walked them to one of the terminals. They all got out safely, but we later heard that there was a leak in the tunnel. I was SO glad Jerry was home safe and had not been on that train!

At the time the earthquake hit, I was standing in front of a cabinet that held my prized cup and saucer collection. As the house began to shake, I put my arms up to steady the cabinet. In retrospect, that may have been a foolish gesture because the cupboard and glass could have easily come down on me and hurt me, but, my first instinct was to save my collection.

Rocky was fine, but Alyssa became hysterical, and Miguel and Dale thought it was funny and were laughing. Jerry tried to calm them all down. Once things settled down again at the house, Jerry and I left for the seminar in Menlo Park, oblivious to how severe the earthquake had been and all the turmoil it was causing.

We had the radio on while we drove and heard that seismographs logged the quake as a 6.9 on the Richter Scale. The governor had called for a State of Emergency. The Nimitz freeway, especially the Cypress structure, and sections of the Bay Bridge had completely collapsed. There were damages to buildings and other structures, and some locations were in flames! As the news became more current, we learned that the quake was responsible for 63 deaths and 3,757 injuries. It was quite a shock to hear of all the loss – and very frightening.[4]

We reached the magazine headquarters to find that while fifty booths had been set up, most were empty. People had panicked and left the building, anxious to go to their homes. It was like a deserted ghost town, with only a few sponsors remaining in the building picking up merchandise. It left us with an eerie feeling. We drove home in silence.

The next morning, Jerry got a phone call at 5:00 AM. It was one of the executives from Chevron asking him to come to the office to help implement their seventy-two-hour emergency plan.

---

[4] Anonymous. "1989 Loma Prieta earthquake." Wikipedia. Last Modified June 8, 2016. Last accessed June 14, 2016. http://en.wikipedia.org/wiki/1989_Loma_Prieta_earthquake.

The command center had been established, and emergency generators were brought in to use as power sources. Media announcements told most of the employees to stay home for at least three days and wait until further notice. Executives responsible for the continued functioning of the company and key office and facility management employees were still working. Some Chevron employees were stuck in their offices for a few hours after the quake. The main building was an old 1922 brick building and some of the bricks had fallen. Rubble eight to ten inches deep was around the perimeter of much of the building and in the garage. Some exits were blocked. Jerry put light sticks down to provide enough light for service trucks to enter and exit the garage. It was quite a mess, but, fortunately, no one in the garage was injured.

The chauffeurs used Cadillacs like four-wheel drive cars to get the executives over the rubble to get to their offices. Even driving in the streets was difficult due to the debris. There was broken glass piled up as high as the curbs on some streets. Chevron volunteered the use of their cars to the SF police and fire departments, along with batteries and barrels of diesel fuel. Jerry was proud to be part of a socially conscientious company that was willing to assist like that in an emergency.

22. Anita 'N Sue

One of Jerry's friends at Chevron was from Europe. He invited us to go with his family to the Netherlands on a guided tour through five countries. One of our first experiences there was attending a birthday party. We found it interesting that in the Dutch tradition, *all* family members receive a gift at the party. Their feeling is that the person of honor made it to that age due to the love and support of family and friends. The gifts were a way to thank them. It seemed like a nice tradition.

After the party, we went to another family member's home to spend the night. Tini lived in a two-story fairytale style home. Before retiring for the night, Tini asked Jerry if he would like a douche. Knowing what the word douche means in America, Jerry was surprised and asked, "What may I ask is that?"

Trying to think of the word to translate it for us, Tini answered, "Well…Um…! It's a bath, of course!" We had a good chuckle, and Jerry took a nice warm bath.

After a few days of staying with Tini, our group of ten people met in Delft. The drive took us into Germany, Austria, and, as it was known then, Yugoslavia. We also had the opportunity to tour some of the islands in the Adriatic Sea. We were told that Brach was where most of the white marble was purchased for building the White House in Washington, D.C.!

The next two weeks we traveled to several cities and small villages. We saw a building in Split, where Julius Caesar ruled at one time. It was made of beautiful marble covered in gold. I'd never seen anything like it before!

While in the midst of Roman era ruins, we noted that we were in the location of the beginning of a civil war. It was all very interesting to get a view of history from a close vantage point.

Later that week we went to one of the Yugoslavian villages where all the streets were made of uneven stone. It was said the rocky streets were to keep the women from looking upward. Women were bartered for, bought, and sold in this part of the country. The tour guide demonstrated this, using Jerry and me as an example. He asked Jerry if he could buy me with six rugs and three camels. Jerry went along, saying he wanted ten rugs and six camels. The guide said yes, because I was full of spunk and he liked the color of my burgundy-red hair. Once the bartering was done, the man who "purchased" me quickly scooped me up and threw me over his shoulder. He carted me up to his bedroom. I wasn't quite sure what to expect at that point, but I wasn't going to let anything personal happen! I started screaming and the man began to laugh. He opened the door and let Jerry in. I guess our travel companions had a good laugh over that joke! It was fun, but a bit unnerving to think that at some point in time this was a typical way of doing things in that culture.

The next stop was in Mostar to see the arched marble bridge that was completely bombed in the civil war. Following that, we went to Dubrovnik. The bus trip took us over the Austrian Alps where we saw a statue that is dedicated to the victims of the Concentration camps of World War II. There was a bone-chilling feeling of horror as we heard about the mistreatment of so many people who tragically lost their lives in the Holocaust. Many of us were brought to tears as we gained newfound respect for those lost souls.

We caught our flight back to the U.S. in Amsterdam. It had been a wonderful experience. Now we were hooked on travel!

Of course we still needed to work to pay for all the trips we wanted to take. I worked for several years as a supervisor in charge of merchandising and management at the Save Mart in San

Jose. In addition, I was still involved in the travel industry.

I loved to spread my wings to see what I was capable of doing. By 1991, the pharmacist at Save Mart had moved to a Walgreen's Pharmacy. One day he called and offered me a position as a pharmacy technician. I was doing well at Save Mart, but an opportunity in the medical field was very appealing to me. I gave my two-week notice and went to Walgreens. They immediately sent me for training. My personal experience with my parents' and Rocky's medical conditions and medications gave me an advantage in learning details about prescriptions, dosages, side effects, and drug interactions. It appeared I had a natural aptitude for the job. The head pharmacist even suggested that with my level of knowledge and personal experience I could bypass the college degree requirement and attend a pharmacy school in Idaho for two years. That would allow me to become a full-fledged pharmacist. Walgreens would pay for my expenses! I was flattered that he had so much confidence in my abilities and truly appreciated the opportunity being offered. If I did follow that path, it would mean either being away from my family for most of the two years, or uprooting them to Idaho. I didn't feel comfortable with either option, so I declined the offer.

The medical field was very interesting to me. I learned a lot more about prescriptions, and I enjoyed interacting with the public. At times, however, it was difficult. I felt so badly when I had to tell a customer who was obviously in pain that it was too soon to refill their pain medication, or that their insurance would not cover it. Many people could not afford to pay out of pocket.

My career as a pharmacy tech was abruptly interrupted one day. As I crossed the parking lot after lunch, I was hit by a car! I was thrown into a half somersault, landing on the ground in a sitting position in front of the car. Naturally, the driver couldn't see me as I was now below her line of vision. She was revving her engine, trying to get over whatever resistance was keeping her car from moving along smoothly. At that point, she didn't realize *I* was that resistance! Luckily for me, a man in the Subway store saw what was happening and rushed out to stop the driver from running completely over me! She claimed she didn't see me walking across the parking lot. An ambulance was called and I was taken to the hospital. I was there for several hours. The doctor wanted to keep me overnight for observation, but I insisted on being released so that I could go home. Jerry was notified and picked me up. There was concern that I might have a concussion, and that my thinking might not be one hundred percent – not a good thing for an important job filling people's prescriptions. The doctor told me not to return to work for at least seven to ten days.

When I did return to work, there had been a change of management in the pharmacy. In addition to working behind the prescription counter, I was now also asked to work floor duty with over-the-counter medications and supplies. One day an elderly man came to pick up a pain medication for his wife. That particular day he did not have the full amount owed for the prescription. He was distraught. His wife was suffering with cancer. I told him to wait a minute and went to get my purse. The pharmacist on duty saw what I was doing, and told me that we could *not* give any customer financial aid. If I did, I would lose my job. No one had ever cautioned me about this before or said what the repercussions would be for either me or the department. It hit me so hard having to tell the gentleman that he couldn't have the medication. The pharmacist called the store manager over to report the incident. He started yelling at me for even thinking of doing something that could jeopardize the department, and possibly the store. He wrote me up. I called in sick the next few days and then handed in my resignation. I couldn't handle the feeling of helplessness, that I wasn't allowed to spare a little of my own personal money to help someone in need.

Jerry told me we needed to go on a vacation so I could get over it. The warm weather, change of scenery, and social time would help me regroup. We decided to take a trip to Southern California with our friends Sue and Hunter. During the trip, Sue and I talked about our desires to start our own businesses. I loved doing crafts, especially designing and making floral arrangements. Lucy, another contact from my days at the grocery stores, ran a side floral business working out of her house. She knew I enjoyed the creativity involved in doing crafts and had been kind enough to give me any supplies she had left over. She taught me a lot about design and business.

Sue was also into homemade crafts. We decided to become partners and start our own company to market our floral arrangements and other handmade craft items. As we contemplated various names for our business, we looked for something with a warm, personal sound. Our husbands suggested we just call it Sue and Anita's Creations. We liked the idea, but thinking about marketing and which name would show first in the phone book, we altered it a bit to *Anita 'n Sue's Creations*.

Sue's main focus was pillows, scarves, and blankets. I was more into home décor pieces like floral garlands and wreaths. We set up a booth at flea markets, church events, and any small venue where we had the opportunity to sell our merchandise. It was an attempt to get our name into the business sector and we hoped we could build a solid customer base. After three months, Sue and her husband decided not to continue with the venture and she signed over her interest in the business to me. It was established as a home-based business, and I wanted to keep it going. Jerry knew it was one of my dreams to have my own business, so he said he would help me on weekends. He became the new "Sue!" Women would ask if he was *A Boy Named Sue,* like the Johnny Cash song. He was a good sport and went along with it. They loved him, and he seemed to enjoy the interactions. He could sell just about anything to anyone!

My daughter Linda was also a big help. She helped set up our show booths at fairgrounds, street fairs, and Christmas Tree Farms. She also helped with designing and making merchandise. I really appreciated her assistance as my business expanded. While I had originally wanted to have my own store, I soon decided it might be more cost effective to rent spaces in different shops rather than have my own brick and mortar store. I started with booths in two shops, expanding over the next five years to fourteen shops! I had anywhere from one to five booths per shop. It was challenging to keep them all stocked and managed, but I loved it.

We made good money, met many nice people, and enjoyed what we were doing. I became known for my handmade wreaths, swags, and garlands. Most were seasonal and holiday items, or for weddings and funerals. Over time, I expanded the variety of merchandise by including general home décor. Before I knew it, I was buying supplies by the pallet in order to make enough items to keep the booths stocked and fill customer requests! I am forever grateful to Lucy for having inspired me to follow my dream.

23. The Great Revealing

Life continued the next few years with Jerry and I both working, taking care of Rocky and our kids, and enjoying each other. My life had been full of many changes in employment, relationships, and responsibilities. 1992 proved to be one of the more significant years of enlightenment for me.

Connie, whom you may remember from the earliest chapters in this book, had tried to be very involved in my childhood and teen years. My parents told me she was my aunt. She had moved away and I hadn't seen her for several years. Both my parents had passed away by this time. Connie called one day saying she was very ill and asked us to come see her in Washington. I didn't really want to go. I resented her attempts to control my life earlier, and, for reasons I will elaborate on later, I didn't trust her. Jerry, being the thoughtful person he is, suggested that I would not want to have any regrets after she was gone, so we should go visit her.

We drove to her home in Tacoma, WA, where she lived with her husband. Soon after we arrived, she tried to persuade me to give her money, mentioning that my mother, Ruth, owed her money and that as the surviving daughter, I was obligated to pay her on my mother's behalf. It seemed that Connie hadn't changed a bit. From my perspective, she was manipulative, and it felt like I was just another dollar sign for her. Her request brought back childhood memories of seeing my mother give Connie hundreds of dollars. I never really understood why Mom and Dad worked so hard to make ends meet, yet always gave money to Aunt Connie. I was told that Connie needed it for this or that, and since she was family, my mother wanted to help her.

My inclination that day might have been to give her a little money now that Jerry and I were better off financially and could spare a bit without impacting our finances too much. Jerry took me aside and commented, "This can't be right. Don't offer to give her any money." Jerry was a neutral party in this situation, and I trusted his instincts. He was able to show me that she had been taking advantage of my family for years. I could see that if I continued giving her money, Connie would continue to take advantage of me indefinitely.

The visit got more "interesting" as the day progressed. If you recall from my childhood experiences with family members, I suspected that Ruth and Joseph were not my birth parents. I did, however, sense a mysterious connection with Connie. I also felt I looked like her more than I did Ruth.

At one point, Connie stood at the kitchen sink washing dishes. I was sitting at the table drinking coffee. She turned around with a quizzical look on her face and asked, "Are you ok? How are you doing?"

"I'm doing fine."

Jerry had been encouraging me to ask Connie about my biological father, so when she asked how I was doing, I took the opportunity. I looked at her and said, "I have a question I'd like to ask you. I've had a feeling for a long time that Ruth and Joseph were not my true parents, and I've been trying to find out more about that. I *think* I know who my mother is... But, I have no clue about my father." Connie stopped what she was doing and looked at me. I knew, just *knew,* she was going to say, "*I* am your mother."

She did indeed say those very words. I felt numb. Could this be real? Could I have been right all along? Was there some underlying reason Connie chose to tell me the truth at this particular time in our lives? Was it because she was ill and thought she was going to die soon? Did she finally want me to know the truth? Or was it just another attempt at manipulation?

She uttered no words of apology, only reasons. She told me that Ruth was actually my great-aunt, and said that Ruth and Joseph needed me. They had gone through a lot since Rocky's birth with four miscarriages and one stillborn child. They really wanted a second child to love. In addition, there was a practical reason. With the health issues Rocky has, and the fact they were older parents, they wanted to make sure there would be someone to care for him after they were gone.

When one hears the parents who raised you are not your real birth parents you most likely assume that you were adopted. I soon learned this was *not* the case for me. There were no adoption papers to document that Connie had given me up at birth and put me into Ruth's and Joseph's loving care. As I continued to ask questions, Connie seemed very bothered. She tried to distract me by suggesting we go for a walk. We didn't get far before my husband and hers met up with us, and that ended that topic of conversation. By this time, I realized that when I had seen Mom giving Connie money, Mom must have felt obligated to pay her for her "gift" and in order to keep the family secret. I felt like I had been sold. I wanted to know more about how this could have happened and why. We left Connie's that night with a few answers and many new questions.

WHAT NEXT???

24. Sisters??

In spite of what Connie said about Mom owing her money, I really did not feel obligated to take care of her. I also had serious reservations. I didn't relish the thought of being at her beck and call! Besides, she had raised six other children. They could take care of her. The real reason went beyond that. I didn't trust her.

Over the years, I had learned that trusting what Connie said was not a good idea. There was the tall tale about her getting inheritance from the woman she had helped; inheritance that never materialized. If I hadn't listened to her, I would have continued to be a better student. Who knows what that difference may have made in my life?

When I became an adult, she asked Jerry and me for money. Having seen how often my parents sacrificed their earnings by giving her money, I had become resentful that she never reciprocated by helping my parents in any way. We never got *anything* from her but elaborate stories and more requests for financial support.

She had *always* wanted my family to take care of her family and their problems. One of her daughters-in-law was murdered. Connie had her son call us, then *she* got on the phone and asked us for two thousand dollars to help pay for funeral expenses. To begin with, the idea of murder made me feel very uneasy. It was a gruesome murder. The police had no idea who the killer was, and the circumstances seemed very vague. No information was given to the rest of the family. There were too many unanswered questions. I told Connie I didn't have that kind of money. Until we bought the new house in 1984, I had been sending her money orders when she requested help. Now that we had a mortgage, I could no longer afford to give her money. She responded, "Well, if *you* don't have the money, I'm sure Jerry does." She assumed that because we were both working, had our own home, and had two rental homes, 'he must be rich.' She asked to talk to Jerry. He knew little about Connie other than she had been calling me every few months asking for money. Jerry gave me a look as he took the phone, and I motioned "no" by nodding my head. Somehow he missed my body language. He assumed that since *I* had been helping her out before, I would want him to help too. He agreed to loan them the two thousand dollars. It took a long time for them to repay him, but the son did repay Jerry. I resented that Connie used her influence to more or less go over my head and borrow money from my husband.

Not long after Connie told me that she was my biological mother, she told my half-siblings as well. They were all very upset with *me,* although to this day I really don't understand why.

I suddenly remembered that one of Connie's daughters, Randy, had told me when we were kids that we were sisters. I thought we were just playing, so I didn't think anything about it at the time. Now I was disappointed that she really must have known and hadn't brought it up again when we were older. I presume she was not allowed to talk about the fact that her mother was also my mother. As children, I don't know if she knew WHY I was being raised by Ruth and Joseph.

My relationship with Connie's youngest daughter, Barbara, changed once the secret that we were actually half-sisters was revealed. She was six years older than Linda, and only eight years younger than me. Before Jerry and I were married, she came over on weekends to spend time with me and the kids. She fit right into the family. She loved my kids, and the feeling was mutual. She was a big help if I needed a babysitter, and was fun to have around. She and I developed a close friendship. We went dancing at the local nightclubs and looked out for each other. She told me that when she got married and had children, she wanted me to be Godmother to them because she felt I would always have their best interests at heart.

A couple of years later, Barbara got married. I helped her plan the wedding and reception, and we had a great time. When she had her son, she asked me to be his Godmother. She always expected me to be there for him. When I could, I treated him like one of my own children, but with five children, sometimes I couldn't do as much for him as what Barbara wanted.

After Barbara heard the news that Connie was also my birth mother, it felt as though she was on edge any time she was around me. She started thinking of possible ideas about who my birth father could be. She even came up with the idea: what if Connie had been raped by a family member? If that was true, then I could be a child of incest. I didn't want to consider that possibility! There were other scenarios, too. It seemed to me that she was somewhat obsessed with that kind of thinking. So far, thankfully, nothing has substantiated any of those ideas.

Barbara's reaction to hearing we were actually half-sisters felt to me like she was abandoning our relationship, one that was important to me. We were raised to believe we were cousins, but, I felt closer to her. In my mind, she felt like a sister. She had helped me escape from Jack by risking her own safety to get the police. I thought that indicated she really cared about me. I guess I was wrong. It made me angry and hurt at the same time.

25. The Investigation Begins

Jerry and I returned from Tacoma. The confirmation of my suspicions was starting to sink in. I wanted to know more about my birth. It appeared that everything was done hush-hush. How was it possible that this situation could have occurred? I had noticed the difference in the parent signatures on the birth certificates. My thoughts are that when Connie entered the hospital when she was in labor, she signed Ruth's name rather than her own. At that time, forms of identification did not have to be shown for admission to a hospital. People just signed in, and it was assumed they were who they said they were. When Connie went home from the hospital, she must have handed me over to my new mother, Ruth.

I began interviewing people who knew Ruth and Joseph well. I told them what Connie had told me, and asked, "Can you verify that I am her daughter?"

People would answer, "No, that can't be right. I saw your mother, Ruth, pregnant with you. I am certain she was pregnant." They really may have seen Ruth pregnant, but not with me. With all those miscarriages I wondered if I might have been a replacement for the last child. Maybe the timing was such that Ruth and Connie were pregnant at the same time. It could have been an opportune time for Connie to give me up without arousing suspicion from neighbors and friends. Ruth's body shape would still look as though she just had a baby, so she could have pretended I was the baby she had delivered. It is a mystery to think Connie could have kept her own pregnancy hidden, but anything is possible.

I still had a lot of questions, even about the accuracy of the birth certificate I had found. Was it the real certificate, or one that was fabricated? Both my birth and Connie's marriage seemed to have taken place in San Francisco, so Jerry and I went to the Hall of Records there. I was able to obtain another certified copy of my birth certificate. It matched the one I found at home, so I was no further ahead on that mystery.

Connie and the husband I knew as a child had split up, and she remarried in the late 1950's. I thought perhaps there might be some information on that marriage certificate to help me answer some of the new questions. We were able to get the certificate and I saw that the age stated on her marriage certificate was twenty-eight, but the age on my birth certificate is twenty-nine. That doesn't seem out of place until you realize that the year of *that* marriage was 1958. I was six years old then! Something was definitely fishy! Again, I left with more questions than answers.

Next, I wanted to talk to my brother Rocky. I wanted to be certain that Connie was telling me the truth about being my birth mother because I had learned over time how deceitful she could be, and how many of her promises were just fabricated stories. Was this just another of her lies? Rocky was eighteen when I was born, so he would remember what happened to at least some degree. He may have a lot of medical issues, but I knew he would be honest, and I trusted him. When I told him what I had discovered, he began to cry. He had overheard adults in the household talk when I was born. They said that my real father was a sailor from Europe, not the man Connie was married to at the time. Apparently the adults decided it would not be a good idea for my biological father to know about me, so he was never told I even existed. I don't know for sure if she was divorced from her first husband at the time I was conceived. They may have been separated. In those days, things like that were not to be acknowledged publicly. It was supposed to be a secret only known to family members. If Connie's husband was not my father, it may explain why I was treated by relatives as an outcast. Was I really the result of an affair Connie might have had while out of town one weekend? I will probably never know for sure.

Rocky had known all my life that Ruth was not my birth mother, but they made him promise not to say anything. In all our forty years together as brother and sister, he never let on. Now he was afraid I would send him away because he wasn't really my brother so I didn't really have to take care of him. But, how could I be upset with *him*? He was an innocent bystander. He was the person I'd grown up with, taken care of, and loved! I tried to reassure him, saying "It's not your fault. You kept the secret as you were told to." Then I added, "It just tells me you know how to keep a really good secret." I smiled at him, and then he knew that things would be alright. We would still be together as a family, and he would continue to be taken care of and loved.

A few months later, Connie called me, asking once again if I would come take care of her. At least this time, she wasn't asking for money. I told Connie that I had Rocky and Jerry, and wouldn't leave them to come take care of her. I wouldn't think of uprooting them either. I suggested she ask her other children. In my mind, she had chosen them to be her family. She had given me up with all the rights that went with it. Why should I be the only one to take care of her now? I felt no obligation to take care of this person who had taken advantage of my real parents, the ones who raised me to be a loving, caring person, and who truly loved me for who I am. They wanted a relationship with me as a person, not because I might have money.

Years ago, a medicine woman had told Connie that if she told me the truth, our relationship would end. It was true. That phone call was our last contact with each other. Several years later, one of Connie's sisters-in-law called to tell me that she had died. She recommended that I not attend the funeral. For a time, I had no contact with any other members of that side of the family. Today, Connie's sister Rachel and her brother Ben have renewed contact with me. Ben has apologized for the family treating me like someone born on the wrong side of the family tree.

Do I forgive them? The answer is yes. I think it is in my soul to forgive a wrong that has been done to me. Forgetting is the hardest to do, and takes the longest to achieve, but I believe that things happen for a reason. If I forget it all, I might miss an opportunity to learn a lesson in life, or find something out about myself. My history is part of what has made me the person I am today. One thing I have learned is that it doesn't matter what situation or problem we have, we can get through it. It is not the things that happen to us that makes the biggest difference. It is how we react to them. We can learn from and overcome obstacles. We all experience failure at one time or another. When we pay attention, we can learn from those failures and use the lessons they hold to grow. Failure can also lead us to appreciate the good things more when life is going well. Success is not measured by what one has or how others see us, but how we feel about ourselves. It's up to us to follow our individual paths, fulfill our own dreams, and seek personal happiness and satisfaction in life.

26. Everyone Pays a Price

Back on the home front, Alyssa, age nineteen, had moved out and blessed us with our granddaughter Deeann. They lived with the baby's father and his mother.

Life continued to be challenging with Dale. He was still very rebellious and getting into trouble. Now that he was in his early twenties, we told him he needed to find another place to live. He went to live with Miguel. We told Dale he was not allowed to be anywhere on our property or in the house. He still seemed to want revenge for something. Jerry was his target, possibly because he knew that hurting Jerry would hurt me more than almost anything else. When Jerry and I were gone for a few days, Dale had a buddy enter through the master bath window and steal things that could be sold or traded for drugs. Everything that was stolen belonged to Jerry, including his antique model car collection and collectible coins. We filed a report with the police and told them we had an idea who was behind the burglary. They got fingerprints, but they couldn't do much without more evidence. They needed to catch them with the stolen items before they could arrest them.

The police were able to help us recover some of the stolen items from pawn shops and places that sold collectibles. Unfortunately, we had to buy the items at the price they had paid Dale or his accomplice, but at least we got some of them back.

Alyssa originally hadn't been happy that Jerry and I had gotten married, but by this time she realized that Jerry was going to stay and would be there for our family. She had come to appreciate what a good person he is, and see the efforts he made to be a good stepdad. When she heard about the burglary, she said, "Oh, my God, Jerry, I'm so sorry." A few weeks later, when she saw that Jerry was still sad about the loss, she decided to work with the police in a sting effort to get more of the stolen items back. She called Dale's friends, telling them she was going to pay a reward to anyone who could help her find the coins and collectible cars. The friends said they knew where some of the items were and they would bring them to her. Naturally, they wanted to collect the reward. They agreed to meet in a strip mall parking lot. The police set Alyssa up with a hidden microphone and hid close by. The friends arrived and she gave them the $250 reward. During the recorded conversation, it came out that one of them had a knife, so the police decided to delay the arrest until Alyssa was safely away from the group. Once she was completely out of the area, the officers recovered Alyssa's money and a few more of the stolen items.

When the sting was over and done, Jerry asked me what I wanted to do about Dale. In order for the police to prosecute Dale, we would have to press charges against him. I felt he needed to be held accountable for his actions, even if it meant spending time in prison. It seemed that, so far, the judges never did much and Dale had been getting off the hook. Part of my concern now was: if he stole from a family member, would he do it to someone else?

I felt we had to make some important decisions, and I relied heavily on Jerry for support. I couldn't do this alone. Dale needed to see that there were consequences for his behaviors. We hoped in the long run our decisions might make such an impression on him that he would get started on a better path. It's called tough love, and, boy, was it tough on all of us! It was one of the most difficult decisions I have ever made, and I've had plenty to make over the years. I decided to press charges against Dale for Grand Theft. It seemed the only way to get the point across that his behaviors were not acceptable to our family or in society.

Typical sentencing time for Grand Theft is three to five years. Maybe spending some time in prison would allow him to come clean from the drugs he was taking, and to think about how his actions were causing us pain and heartbreak.

The Three Strikes Law was in effect in California. The charge of Grand Theft counted as one strike. Future offenses could be counted as more strikes. He knew he could potentially end up in prison for life. He pled guilty. It seemed he had finally hit bottom, and fear struck his heart.

Dale was sentenced to prison. Before he was transferred to the prison facility, he asked Jerry and me to have a doctor write a letter requesting that he be allowed to be imprisoned in the bay area rather than sent elsewhere. He figured if he was close by, Jerry and I would visit him. We had no intention of visiting him in prison because we wanted him to feel the emptiness he had caused us. But, we got a letter from a doctor as he requested. We knew it was unlikely it would make a difference. No surprise, even with the letter, the prison board denied the request.

Because this was more or less a first offense in the court system, the legal system didn't really know where to place Dale. They sent him to two different state prisons, both housing hard core inmates. He eventually ended up in a third one in Corcoran, California, several miles north of Bakersfield. That prison had a substance abuse treatment program. There is usually an initial period of time required during which rehab patients are not allowed contact with friends or family. He had no visitors or contacts with his old life in Fremont. Once that period was over, Jerry and I still did not visit him. I felt it was important for him to experience a short period of being completely away from family to understand the full impact imprisonment could have on his life. My thinking was that if he missed his family, he might be more motivated to change his life. If he didn't miss us, then family didn't mean much to him. If that was the case, then what *was* important to him? He would have plenty of time to work on cleaning up his life, and to learn how to cope with his addiction.

It was a scary time for Dale. He was afraid of being beaten up by other prisoners. In an effort to spend less time with the general prison population, he started going to the prison library. It was one of the best things he could have done. During his two-year imprisonment he earned his General Education Diploma (GED). The drug abuse program didn't work for everyone, but, luckily, it did for Dale. It looked like he might be turning around!

When Dale was released from prison, he lived in a half-way house near our Fremont home. It was a fresh start, but one with its own share of difficulties. When Christmas came and we went to visit him, the other residents locked him up in a shed. Their plan was to withhold food, heat, and blankets. It was a cruel hazing incident. The other housemates did not have family support or friends, and we assumed they were jealous.

Dale managed to break out of the shed and appeared at our doorstep. I had a rule that he could not stay with us at all, so when we opened the door he quickly told us, "I'm not here to stay with you, I just have to get away from that house! I've already contacted another half-way house in Berkeley. I hear it's really tough, but I plan to go there in the morning. I've already been accepted into the program." He was scared, but it seemed he really did want to change. He didn't like the person he had become, and did not want to continue life as a drug addict. We allowed him to spend that night with us.

The new half-way house was very rigid. It was a lot of hard work for Dale, but it turned into a positive, life-changing experience. He was required to keep a journal, and to look back at things he had done so far in his life. He was forced to see all the wrongs he had committed, all the people he had hurt, and try to figure out WHY he had behaved the way he did. No excuses were acceptable.

He was not allowed any visitors, phone calls, or letters for the first sixty days. Residents were to attend church twice a week. After the probation period, we could, and did, take part in the program by attending a family support group. Part of the focus was on how the family had also been victimized by this illness that affects so many people. If Dale had followed the rules the preceding week and demonstrated good behavior, he could join us briefly for a visit during the meeting. We were not allowed to touch him, but we could talk to him. Month by month, we could see a noticeable change in him.

One of the requirements of the program was that participants had to work around the rehab house. After a few months, they were also expected to get paying jobs to reimburse expenses incurred while living there. A percentage of their pay was automatically deducted from their salary. In this phase of rehabilitation, he met and developed a relationship with Carolyn, another resident at the half-way house. When they completed the program, they lived near us for a short time. Then they moved to New Mexico to live near Carolyn's family. Soon they were married and lived with Carolyn's two children from a previous marriage, Eve and Greg. Dale was on his way to a new life and starting his own family.

Carolyn and Dale had two children of their own, Kenny and Patricia. They have since divorced, but remain close friends. Dale sees his children as often as he can. During Dale's years as a teenager and drug addict, we had told him numerous times that being a parent is not easy. Now, having two children who have special needs, and being involved with Carolyn's other children, he has confessed to us, "Now I understand what you were saying to me all the time." He can see how difficult it was for Jerry being a stepfather, and has experienced the complexities of having a blended family from the perspective of parenthood. We like and appreciate the person he has become today.

Dale has started his own computer repair business and is partners with another fellow in a sign making venture. As a voluntary act of repentance, he began saving collectible coins and model cars to replace some of what he stole from Jerry. Our relationship is being rebuilt. We are learning to appreciate and genuinely like each other. He calls us frequently, and we enjoy being able to communicate more comfortably. Little by little we are working toward building a mutual sense of trust.

27. Alyssa and Miguel: Their Journeys

Most parents feel that what happens to their children continues to be important to them, too. We love them from the day they are born, protect them as children, and try to instill good values in them. For me, stepchildren are equally important. Our love and concern doesn't stop when they reach adulthood and move out to forge ahead on their own. We are willing to be there emotionally to support them.

In her teen years, Alyssa had gone to a religious summer camp sponsored by the Mormon Church and felt comfortable with their teachings. I had learned about many religions over the years because Mom and Dad allowed me to explore various belief systems. I wanted my children to have that same freedom. Jerry agreed with me that each of our children should make their own choices when it came to their religious preferences. As in our household, family is highly revered in most religious cultures. Getting involved in church activities seemed to suit Alyssa at the time. Her family was a high priority in her life. She worked hard to be independent and support herself and Deeann.

When Alyssa was twenty-two years old, life threw her a curve ball. She became very ill. Deeann was only three years old and, as any mother can tell you, toddlers need a lot of care, so she and Alyssa moved in with us. We could help care for Deeann. We were very distraught when Alyssa was diagnosed with cervical cancer. She was so young! Doctors told us that the cancer was very aggressive in Alyssa's case, and if she did not have treatment soon, she could die. The doctor performed a radical hysterectomy and removed more than forty lymph nodes. Recovery would be somewhat involved due to the change in hormone levels in her body, in addition to the body's adjustment to fewer protective lymph nodes. Fortunately, the operation was a success. We are all very grateful to the doctor for saving her life. It's been over twenty years now and the cancer has not returned.

A few years later, Alyssa met Ryan. They hit it off and were married in Hawaii two and a half years later. Ryan also had a toddler, Troy, so they became a family of four. Ryan worked as a driver for a big corporation, and Alyssa took continuing education classes to become an insurance claims adjuster.

While Alyssa was getting settled into married life, Miguel was in his mid-twenties. He'd always been a bit of a lone wolf. He did not let others influence him or his decisions. He was usually clear-headed and made wise decisions, so we rarely had to worry about him. He attended a few courses at the local college and found work as a supervisor in the lumber department for a large warehouse store chain.

Life seemed to be going well for him, but every life is faced with challenges. He reconnected with the girl he had gone with in high school. She was pregnant and in trouble. He still had feelings for her and wanted to help in some way. He stayed with her through the pregnancy. She gave birth to a healthy son, and Miguel loved him as if he were his own. When the baby was almost two years old, his drug addicted father came back into their lives. High on drugs one night, he killed the little boy. Both the mother and Miguel were devastated and soon parted ways. The baby's death hit Miguel especially hard, and he grieved for several years.

Some time later, Miguel met Kirsten. She successfully ran her own business and was a beautiful person. Tragically, one rainy day while driving on a freeway overpass, she lost control of her vehicle. The car hit the embankment with such force that she died instantly. This was another serious hit to Miguel's emotions.

Recovery took a very long time.

Jerry and I admire Miguel's ability to stick to his job and never give up. He met Christine, who has three children from a previous relationship, and they decided to live together. Soon, Miguel, Jr. was born. Jerry and I accepted Christine's children as our own grandchildren, and we enjoy keeping in touch with them. We hope Miguel has a long life with his family. I can't help but feel that finding Christine and her children was God's way of giving Miguel something good to balance out all the sorrow he has experienced.

28. Opportunities of a Lifetime

As for new events in my life, in the mid-nineties I rented several spaces in a shop called the Boutique Gallery in Newark. The two couples who owned the shop knew my reputation as an established entrepreneur. When they decided they wanted a silent partner to help with financial support in the store, and to bring in more merchandise, they approached me. It seemed to be a good opportunity, so I helped them with money on an "as needed" basis, and purchased more merchandise for the store. After several months, the couples felt their expenses were exceeding the income needed to maintain the business. They decided they needed to reverse that tactic and downsize the business. I ambitiously wanted to expand my business, so we parted ways on good terms. The way I thought about it, it had been worth my time and money to get the training and experience.

I still wanted to open and manage my own store. Two other eager women, crafters in their own right, also had booths at a boutique and wanted to own a gift shop. In October, I applied for and was granted a loan of $10,000 to invest in the new business venture. Over the next few months, one of the other partners put in another $10,000. The three of us agreed that since our third partner was unable to provide financial backing, she would work more hours in the store as a trade-off. We made plans to open our shop, which we decided to name Herbs 'N Such. Jerry had to co-sign on the lease since we used our house as collateral. We all met at the store to sign the lease for the building. As I sat on the floor in the middle of the store, I had an awful, sinking feeling. It just came over me. It felt as though the space was shouting out a big 'NO.' I didn't understand it at the time. How could I feel that way when my dream was finally becoming a reality? I should be feeling on top of the world! I thought I was just nervous, as anyone would be taking a big step like that. I chose to ignore the feelings and we signed the lease. In a few days, the store was open for business. We featured floral design and herbal products. I was excited and happy!

Marco and Fay Wong owned a wholesale floral warehouse. They gave us great discounts on the individual floral stems we bought from them. A few times they came to Herbs 'N Such and watched while I intertwined the floral pieces and created arrangements. They asked a lot of questions, including how well our products sold. One day when I went in to purchase more floral supplies from them, they asked me if I would design five original floral arrangements for them to take to China. They wanted to see how well those designs would be accepted in the retail industry. I was happy to fulfill their request. After a few months, they returned from China and reported that four of the five sample pieces had sold very well. They were quite pleased and asked me to create a few more arrangements. As before, they supplied all the materials I needed. Those arrangements were also well received. They contracted with companies in China to have them manufactured in bulk for the retail industry. Little did I know that networking would change my life in the future!

While I was opening up the new business, Jerry continued to work for Chevron. He had been employed by them for thirty-seven years, the last ten working with the executive staff. Chevron offered him a retirement package on more than one occasion. Jerry turned down the first offers, feeling he was too young to retire at fifty-five years of age. In 1996, Chevron decided they needed to downsize and once more offered him the opportunity to leave the company with a generous package. He discussed the offer with me and finally accepted their offer. It was just too good to pass up!

He almost missed the deadline; he got the paperwork turned in ten minutes before the offer expired!

Jerry loved his job, and requested that they include an option for him to be rehired after six months as a consultant if he wanted to return to work. He wasn't really sure what life in retirement mode would be like, or how he would fill his days after years of a very busy schedule. Little did he know we would have no problem finding things to do!

There were five retirement parties for Jerry. He felt like they were treating him "like gold." The CEO hosted one of the parties, and surprised Jerry by arranging for Jerry's parents to come from Portland, Oregon, to attend. The company paid for all their expenses. It was amazing!

Herbs 'N Such did well for a year or so. However, eventually our debts increased, but sales did not. Conflicts among the partners emerged. I wanted to dissolve the partnership, but the landlord fought us about breaking the lease. We had to keep the business going a while longer. Tensions were building.

In order to pay the rent and typical expenses of running a store, I had to find an additional job. Fortunately, I was hired by Ross's Western District Distribution Center to work in the human resources department. After three months, I left Ross and found employment with See's Candies while waiting for a job in the floral department of Safeway. Both See's and Safeway are union shops, which meant the hours worked there could be added to my earlier hours worked in the retail industry. I could stay in the union retirement plan. Even with all the over-time hours I had worked on weekends and holidays at my previous job with Save Mart, I still needed a few more to qualify for a pension. I used the paychecks from these new jobs to pay bills at the store, and hoped to fulfill my goal to get retirement benefits. It was a big effort to add more hours to my work schedule, but I was glad to be gaining potential security for my retirement years.

I was able to keep Herbs 'N Such from going under, but, I could barely make ends meet with all the store expenses. The other partner, who had been putting in money as well, was no longer able to do so. Because Jerry and I had provided the collateral, we had the most to lose. We decided it was time to close Herbs 'N Such, even if it meant breaking the lease. In January of 1999, Jerry and I met with the landlord to discuss the process of closing the store. The earliest we could close would be in March. In order to get out of the last year of the lease, the landlord required that we still pay for six months' rent. Jerry and I wrote a check to him for $6,500. One of the partners had used the business as collateral in order to get a home loan, so I felt it was only fair that she put in the balance of $3,000. We knew that the third partner was unable to contribute.

I was told I could pursue legal action against the partners, but I knew they didn't have the money. As the saying goes, "You can't get blood out of a turnip." I knew it would be a futile effort. I chose to just take it as a financial loss, a lesson to follow my instincts in the future, and to move on. When all was said and done, it turned out to be a $100,000 business loss for Jerry and me. I had to sell my mother's home to pay off all the bills that were left after the store closed. That was particularly difficult because one of our daughters was living there with her husband and children. I knew moving would be a financial hardship for them, and I hated having to tell them to move, but I felt I had no other option to get the money I needed to close the business that was putting me in debt. In one way, it may have been a good time for the move because we learned that our daughter was divorcing her husband. It may have made it easier for them to make the actual separation. After the move, Jerry and I covered most of the initial expenses to help her get on her feet again.

It took two years of struggling to finally get out from under the remaining expenses, and my dream had to be set aside for the time being, but I didn't give up. Someday I would try again!

They say when one door closes, another one opens. Soon after the store closed, a new opportunity was presented to me. One of my former partner's friends, Elizabeth, worked in the Human Resources Department of Gigabyte. She suggested I apply for a job there. I was hired on her recommendation. I didn't even have to fill out a formal application. It seemed almost too easy. I was apprehensive, but thought I would give it a try.

Gigabyte was a company run by two professors from the local University in Palo Alto. In the heyday of the dot-com era they decided to capitalize on the tech business boom by opening a business developing broadband and Wi-Fi technology. They brought engineers from overseas to work on the new technology. The business was quickly taking off. They hired me to design and set up their lobby and offices, as well as expand their employees' cubicles. I bought furniture, partitions, decorations, and food – whatever they wanted. In addition, I helped Elizabeth in the HR Department with shopping for health plans and benefits.

The new job was going well, life was good at home, and I was out of the failing partnership with Herbs 'N Such. All seemed to be going better. Some call it Murphy's Law, but, just when things seem to be improving, something else can happen in our lives to throw us onto the downhill slant of the roller coaster again. Our daughter Linda found herself in an abusive relationship with her husband. She immediately got the marriage annulled. Now, she and her nephew Don were living in Oregon.

She started her own packing company, contracting with large moving van companies. Her employees would pack clients' items in preparation for their move. In addition, she worked for Harry & David, a catalog gift company. One winter day, on her way home from Harry & David, her '83 Ford LTD hit black ice. She swerved to avoid hitting the car ahead, but her car slid over the icy surface into it. Behind her, a huge eighteen-wheel semi-truck was unable to stop in time. It plowed into the back of her car, bouncing her car across the lanes. The driver door was lodged in place and had to be cut open. The front driver's seat had fallen backwards during the first impact, so when the truck hit her, she was in a lying down position. Linda sustained serious back injuries. She was air-lifted to a hospital where she spent several days. When she was released, she couldn't even walk. As soon as she was able to travel, and when our grandson Don would be out of school, Jerry and I drove to Oregon to bring them to Fremont. Linda could live with us while she was recovering from her injuries. Don moved back in with his mom.

Linda was able to walk again, but the injuries she suffered caused lifelong consequences. She had no medical coverage, and she only had basic car insurance at the time of the accident. Her automobile policy in Oregon had a No Fault clause. That meant that regardless of who was really at fault for the accident, each party paid for their own damages. She received no compensation for the car or help with medical bills. Talk about hitting a person when they're down! It took nearly a year for Linda to recover enough physically to look for employment again. Getting jobs was even more difficult because after the accident she could neither stand nor sit for more than ten minutes at a time. That narrowed her options.

Linda took some accounting classes and had some

experience as a bookkeeper. She accepted a job with an income tax preparation company. When they saw the pain and mobility difficulties she had while trying to do her job, they suggested she go to a job rehabilitation center. Those programs are designed to assist people with learning new skills that will help them find full-time employment. She found a local center that paid for job training and provided her with the follow-up medical care she needed. She appreciated that opportunity. Linda has always been responsible and dedicated to her jobs. After leaving the rehab center, she worked for the tax company for ten years.

The job at Gigabyte allowed me to keep flexible hours. Jerry and I were able to check on Linda throughout the work day. Part of my duties at Gigabyte included managing catering for the office. Dealing with ten to twenty different nationalities in one office was not easy! They all had cultural expectations, dietary requirements, and preferences. It became a very demanding job, especially as the company continued to grow quickly over the next few months. They moved their operations from a small rental space in Menlo Park to a 48,000 square foot building in San Jose.

The biggest event I was responsible for was the Christmas party. The CEO's told me, "Do something special. We want a really big smash for Christmas." They wanted the party to be staged on the second floor of the building: 24,000 square feet of empty space! It was going to be a challenge to decorate such a huge, bare, concrete area. With the help of Elizabeth and Jerry, we succeeded in transforming it into a winter wonderland! We decorated seven tall Christmas trees with long, cascading garlands, and I made five-foot wreaths to decorate the walls.

I ordered three hundred boxes of See's candy to be handed out as gifts. On each box I added a gift tag on which I had handwritten each attendee's name. In addition, I was expected to purchase and wrap the personal gifts they were giving to each employee and their guest. One of our friends belonged to a musical group, so we enlisted the lead female vocalist to provide entertainment for the event. No expense was spared. Guests had a wonderful time and my bosses were happy. Jerry and I were exhausted, but I was satisfied and happy that I had successfully managed to oversee such a large event. It was a boost to my confidence.

29. Authentic Chinese Food Anyone?

Early the next year, a headhunter called and wooed me away from Gigabyte where I had worked for ten months or so. I went to another dot-com start-up company to set up their library. The twelve-foot by eighteen-foot room was a jumble of books and merchandise. They wanted *me* to sort out their whole mess! It took a whole month to clean it up and organize it so it was usable as a library. When that job was completed, I'd had enough of cleaning up their mess, so when they asked if I wanted to work on other jobs for them, I declined.

During the month I was tackling the library, Marco Wong called to ask if I would work for him as a designer at American Asia Trading Company. He wanted me to design new products that would have retail appeal and could be sold at the wholesale level at stores here in the U.S. I made several proto-types, experimenting with materials to see which might be most cost effective for the company and the manufacturer. I put together garlands, swags, and groups of arrangements, but also created individual floral stems and greenery. He was pleased when the new prototypes went over well and he soon put them into mass production in China.

The Wong's had a network of associates in China and worked directly with manufacturers. As a creative designer, I was astute at recognizing the quality of products, so I could be an asset when visually inspecting the products at their source in China. I was also good at negotiating and marketing. Marco asked if I would like to go to China to meet the manufacturers and design more for his company. I was leery of being in a foreign country by myself, so my first reaction was, "I can't travel without my husband."

Marco replied, "Not a problem. We'll pay for him to go with you." Since Jerry had retired from Chevron, he *could* go! It was the first of many trips abroad for business. Marco and his wife Fay always accompanied us.

That worked out so well that Marco asked if Jerry and I would be interested in representing his company at gift shows around the United States. He and Fay spoke both Cantonese and Mandarin, and somewhat limited English. We were desirable employees for them because we could explain marketing information to the American companies for them. We weren't sure how the gift show circuit could work for us due to the fact that we couldn't take Rocky with us and he needed someone to look after him at home. Linda was still living with us and offered to take care of her uncle while we were gone. We very much appreciated her offer and decided to give the gift show circuit a whirl.

Our very first show was in San Francisco. Jerry and I set up the ten-foot by thirty-foot temporary display area. As potential buyers stopped to inspect our wares, we would engage them in conversation. Jerry is so good with people! He enjoyed meeting the buyers and taking their orders. Before long, we got used to the routine and the job quickly turned into a full-time position. Twice a year we went on the show circuit, doing eight shows across the country. We traveled from Dallas to Atlanta, then to Philadelphia. Next was Chicago, followed by Las Vegas. Finally, it was back to the West Coast to Los Angeles and Seattle. Our final stop was usually San Francisco. Each show took eight days. We were gone a long time!

With all that travel twice a year, it meant we were away from home six months of the year. Jerry really liked traveling. He was particularly intrigued with the trips to China and being exposed to a different culture, lifestyle, and customs. I wasn't too happy about being gone so much. My idea of traveling was to sit and have fun on a cruise ship! It was hard for me to adapt to this type of travel and lifestyle, but I got used to it.

I've heard that copying is the highest form of flattery, but, a designer wants their work to be recognized as being their original creation. Unfortunately, some manufacturers have copying down to a fine art, and can easily and more cheaply reproduce copies of originals that can be put into the marketplace within one to two months. This became a big source of frustration for us. Competitors would come to the shows and, even though no cameras were allowed, they would have them hidden in their bags and slyly take photos of our displays and merchandise. The wreaths, swags, and garlands were made with silk or acrylic flowers, leaves, and berries that were braided together. Most of the individual stems and floral pieces were sold individually. Displays were intended to suggest ways that the individual pieces could be used. The industry calls them semi-finished products. The secretive buyers would actually push pieces of both individual items and arrangements aside in order to get close-up pictures of the design and see how the items were made. Fay had no patience for it. Marco was diplomatic, saying, "They are still our customers." Fay, however, would physically chase them out of our area, yelling, "Go away! Get out of here!" I always appreciated her attitude and her efforts to respect my creativity and product designs.

On one of our trips to China, I made a prototype and placed an order for several cases of it with a small manufacturing company. When we returned from the trip a month later, the design had already been sold to a competitor and the product was available in stores here in the U.S.! We hadn't received *our* order yet! Someone had taken away the opportunity for me to introduce *my* original creation! I was furious! We never placed an order with *that* manufacturer again!

Unfortunately, Linda had a similar experience with one of the craft products she had created. Her design was copied and reproduced without her permission. It feels like such an invasion of personal rights!

One of the biggest challenges of this job was the "on demand" process of creating new products on short notice. The spontaneity and the need to be innovative stretched my creative abilities. If I could have worked solely in the warehouse design area designing products, the job would have been easier. But the owners also had me speaking to customers on the phone about orders, making sure the orders were filled and ready for shipment via UPS. I was often sent out to design products for customers at their sites.

At that time, Linda was without a job and experiencing financial hardship. We could help her with some expenses, but there were many medical bills. Marco, aware of her situation and physical limitations, offered her a flexible job in the office. It was a Godsend for us all. Even with Linda's help, as the customer base grew by leaps and bounds it was too much responsibility for two people, so Marco hired a few more employees.

During our trips to China we were always accompanied by a liaison who made the appointments for us to meet with the manufacturers and set up our dining and hotel accommodations. They often filled in as interpreters as well. It was a pretty fast-paced trip, visiting twenty-two factories in two weeks. We made a large circle, traveling from Beijing to the north eastern city of Shen Yung, then to Dahlia, a bit east of Beijing. On the way back to Beijing for our return flight home, we visited many small villages.

At the time, we were surprised to see the factories were

not what we are accustomed to seeing here in the U.S. Ours are typically huge buildings with many employees. In China, a factory might be in a big brick building, an elementary school, or even a simple lean-to similar in appearance to a chicken coop. They were all regulated to some extent. We had heard about "sweat shops" that employ young children. One requirement I placed on my employment with the Wong's was that I would *not* tolerate any child labor. If I saw *any* child working, I would not continue to do business with that manufacturer. Fortunately, during our many visits to the factories, we never saw children at work. One might suggest that the factory managers knew we were going to visit, so they hid the children. While I worked on designs in the front of the factory, Jerry went to the back unannounced. We were very happy that he never saw *any* children working in those factories.

It was interesting to us that many of the manufacturing company factories were located above elementary school classrooms. Many schools had five or six stories, so there was enough space for a manufacturer to set up shop on the upper floors. One benefit of being up that high was that no one could look in the windows to see what was being made. The proprietor's designs were protected.

In addition to the privacy afforded the companies in the tall buildings, there were other security measures. Often we had to pass through locked gates that surrounded the factories. When we arrived, a guard would unlock the gate, let us pass through, then lock the gate behind us. He would secure the guard dog to a chain-linked fence so we would not be attacked. The guard then opened all four doors of the car and escorted us into the factory. Uniformed men inside the buildings would withdraw into the background, and a woman receptionist took over for the visit.

On one occasion, a guide approached us when we entered a display room and asked me, "Well, what do you think?"

Although I am an open, very up-front person who usually tells it like it is, I knew that diplomacy was needed in this situation, especially being a visitor in another country. I simply replied, "This is not the type of material I am looking for."

My reply lead to different results than you might imagine. Instead of being offended and escorting us back to our car, we were taken to another room on the second floor! The products on that floor were of better quality. They started asking questions about what type of merchandise we were seeking and what materials we wanted.

Guess what? *Then* they showed us a third room with even higher quality products! I was pleased with these items, so told them I wanted to place an order. We were then taken to their boardroom, which had high quality walnut office furniture and elegant décor. The order was taken using an Abacus (an early calculator used in China). There was no paper work for placing orders like we are used to filling out in the U.S. There was no handshaking either, which in the U.S. under certain circumstances seals a deal. Basically, we just showed them what we wanted, they gave us the price, and, if we agreed, we had to just trust the order would be filled as requested. They notified Marco when the shipment was ready, he paid them, and the product was shipped to him in the States. It was an interesting process, and, to us, a different way of doing business.

It was difficult to have a completed product assembled in only one factory. Many manufacturers were reluctant to share information with each other, so each piece of a product was produced at a different location to preserve the secrecy of the design. For example, if the end product was to be a flower, the stem would be made at one factory, the leaves at another, and the petals at a third. This complicated our job, but we had to learn to cope with it. The alternative to working with several different factories was to use the pieces already produced at one factory. Sometimes that meant compromising part of my design, which was frustrating.

At one particular factory, we made it to the third level and placed a large order. Based on prior experience with other executives, we thought they would be happy and smiling. They remained stand-offish, however. It occurred to Marco that we had arrived in a Lexus, a Japanese made car. We had probably unknowingly committed a cultural faux-pas!

Jerry later read *The Rape of Nanking* by Iris Chang. He learned that in 1937-38 the Japanese invaded the ancient city of Nanking, which was the capital of The Republic of China at the time. An estimated 260,000 Chinese civilians were massacred by the Japanese army. Some of those were women and young girls who were raped and/or mutilated before being killed. One historian estimated that if the dead from those seven weeks of killing were to link hands, their bodies would stretch a span of approximately two hundred miles. The Japanese occupied Nanking for a total of eight years. [5] We had no idea the feelings of animosity that might have arisen from those events carried over to the use of our Lexus for transportation. We assumed that blunder was also the reason our welcome reception had not been as warm as on other trips. Needless to say, we never rented another Lexus again while in China. All in all, our interactions with Chinese countrymen and businessmen were interesting and respectful educational experiences.

---

[5] Iris Chang, *The Rape of Nanking: The Forgotten Holocaust of World War II,* (Basic Books, 1997), 13-14.

As a designer, one of my greatest rewards is seeing my creations featured in the display windows of places like the Wynn Casinos and the Ethel M candy factory in Las Vegas. It is satisfying to know that my creativity and efforts are being viewed, appreciated, and enjoyed by many people.

30. The Golden Years Begin

By now you have read that our life together has not always been a cake walk. Like most couples, we have had our share of challenges, drama, and heartache. In 2002, a few days after we were told that one of our beloved nephews had died in a tragic accident, Jerry was diagnosed with prostate cancer. Tests indicated it was an aggressive form. The prognosis was bleak – two years. He was only sixty-one years old – in our opinion, too young to leave this planet. We were numb with disbelief! I lit a candle at home and made a promise to God to always keep it burning if he would keep the cancer in remission and keep Jerry healthy. We started to attend a support group affiliated with the hospital to learn more about treatment options and hear what others have gone through with their cancer. God must have heard my prayers. Doctors treated the cancer aggressively with hormone treatments to shrink the tumor before adding radiation. I am very happy to say that the results exceeded expectations!

We continue to attend and be actively involved in the support group. The information we learn there about treatment options, nutrition, and medical technology has helped us to make informed decisions and be better able to cope with the situation emotionally. We highly recommend that others newly diagnosed with cancer do what they can to learn about their condition. Look for reading materials, talk to doctors and nurses, ask questions, and seek out the support of others who have been in similar positions.

A few other distressing things happened in the months following Jerry's cancer diagnosis. We lost another loved one, a young daughter-in-law who died unexpectedly from a brain aneurism. Then, a new great-granddaughter died only a couple of weeks after birth. We put our lives on hold and did what we could to deal with whatever came up, and to support other family members who were learning to cope with their tragedies.

After Jerry recovered from his first cancer treatment, he was cleared to travel again. We were ready to be on the road! The doctor suggested going to Italy. He thought it was one part of the world we should see while we could. We asked Jerry's sister Judy and her husband Alden to go with us. They had sadly just lost a loved one in an awful accident and we thought they could use the diversion. Our three weeks together in Italy were wonderful! We began and ended the trip in Rome. There was so much history to see and a new culture to understand.

Jerry's sister and her husband enjoyed the trip so much they asked us to let them know when we planned more trips. The travel bug had bitten them, too. Since the excursion to Italy, we have been to several countries with them and taken trips on our own as well. We have been to some third world nations. Jerry is proud of the fact that he has traveled to sixty-five countries (some twice) and all fifty states in the U.S. My tally is not far behind. Each place has its own flavor and captivating interests.

In addition to our travels, we still worked for Marco. He hired a few more people to help with the expanding business. When he heard about Jerry's cancer, he was very concerned for his health, as well as being generally nervous at even hearing the word cancer. After a few more gift shows, he discussed his concerns with us and suggested it might be time for us to stop doing the heavy work involved in setting up the displays. He felt it was time for us to part ways.

Almost immediately one of Marco's competitors, Bill, asked us to work for him. His business was similar to Marco's, but on a smaller scale. He and his wife ran the company. They had observed how much Marco's business had grown with our help. Once Bill got wind that we were no longer working for Marco, he jumped in and asked for our expertise to give his business a boost. The first project was a trip to China to create more designs and purchase products.

Traveling with Bill presented a few new adventures. On our first trip, I was asked to design a special garland of grapes. That was nothing new for me, as I had designed several of them for Marco. What made this time unique was that the showroom at the manufacturer's factory where I was to create this design had been without power for a couple of months! It was night-time and very dark outside. They brought emergency generators and flood lights in to work by, but it was still very hard to see. As usual, I created the design and the first sample was sent to the factory owner who would offer his price to put them into mass production. If it was too expensive, they brought the product back to me and I tried to figure out how to make the same design with cheaper materials. After a few times of going back and forth, they reached an agreement on the product price.

From there we took an overnight train through a snow blizzard to the port city of Dalian. We were a bit taken aback when we noticed that nearly everyone in the city was wearing surgical masks. They were in the middle of an extremely dangerous and contagious SARS epidemic. We went to the factories there, designed the products, and left as soon as possible the next day.

Our flight had one stop in Shanghai. All 300 passengers were guided to an enclosed area in the airport where they checked our temperatures to make sure we were not suffering from SARS. They shuffled us through in twenty minutes. It was amazing! I was having a hot flash, so I worried I might be detained, but they let me pass through. We were so happy to return home! Coincidentally, that was our last business trip to China.

Two years later, Bill decided he couldn't keep the business. Once again we parted ways as friends with an employer. We did a lot of traveling over the next several years, and I continued my home-based business with sales booths in several stores. Life was good.

As luck would have it, on our roller coaster of life, Jerry tore his Achilles tendon while on a hike in 2012. Rather than perform surgery, doctors decided to keep his foot in a cast for the next three to four months with the hope it would heal on its own. Every two weeks a new cast was put on to change the angle of his foot. They say you can't hold a good man down, and Jerry sure fits that bill. He kept up with as many activities as he could, and by the time he was in an air boot, he went to the Indy 500 in 100 degree weather with some of his friends. He managed to hobble up and down the stairs to their seats in the 250,000 seat venue. Talk about determination!

When Jerry's birthday came near that year, I planned a big party for him. We wanted to celebrate he was still with us and healthy! We went to the Lake Elizabeth Community Center in Fremont. The kids and I made centerpieces with cars, floral accent pieces, and miniature gas pumps. His son Christopher created a full-sized car engine out of Styrofoam and aluminum foil. He even brought a cherry picker to hang the motor in the middle of the room. Car key chains fit in well with the theme as party favors. Shelley, a family member, sang a song for Jerry and me to dance to, and another for the kids and grandkids. It was a very fun day!

In 2013 our daughter Lynn was diagnosed with cancer. I can't tell you how terrifying it is to hear your child has such a life-threatening condition. And this was our second experience with one of our children and cancer! Lynn went through chemo treatments and is now considered cancer free. We are so thankful that we will continue to have her in our lives. It was also a reminder that life is short and we should take every opportunity to enjoy our time with people while we can.

With Linda still at home to be with Rocky, Jerry and I expanded our travels to include leisure travel along with attending gift shows to display and order merchandise for resale in my store booths. The spring following Lynn's treatment, Jerry and I went on a cruise through the Panama Canal with Jerry's sisters Debbie and Judy, and their husbands Tom and Alden. Aunt Pat and Uncle Fritz accompanied us on this trip. They were celebrating their sixty-first wedding anniversary, so it was a very special occasion. Much to everyone's shock, Fritz passed away unexpectedly just a few months later. It was a good reminder not to delay doing things on our bucket list.

In July, Jerry and I planned the traditional week-long family reunion. Jerry has two sisters and one brother, both of whom are married and have their own children, and some have grandchildren. About twenty to thirty adults and children attended and there was a fairly wide range of ages. We figured out a cooking schedule so that each family prepared a meal or two for the whole group. It was fun tasting their favorite dishes. Our creativity to come up with games that might interest everyone was put to the test as we attempted to come up with new activities. We feel fortunate that we have a family willing to get together for a few days annually. In today's society, that is not always the case!

I continued to maintain booths in several stores. I also taught a few classes on merchandising to interested vendors. Jerry and I developed a system for ordering merchandise months in advance, pricing items, and bagging them in attractive wrap to make them more marketable. It was not unusual to come home to find boxes and boxes of merchandise stacked in the living room, waiting to be readied for distribution. I have since relinquished some of my booths, so there aren't so many places to keep stocked with merchandise, but there is still plenty to keep me busy. Part of the agreement for renting space in some stores is to participate by actually working in the store a specified number of days each month. Fortunately, I only do store work hours now at one store in San Jose. Otherwise, working in several stores could be a full-time job, and I need time to shop for and prepare merchandise for display as well as seeing to Rocky's care and managing our home.

A few years ago, I stopped making floral arrangements for commercial purposes. The repetitive motions involved in twisting the wires and applying pressure to secure pieces together was getting hard on my wrists, hands, and fingers. Instead, I decided to focus on purchasing a variety of other gift merchandise, from porcelain animals and plush teddy bears, to items with a musical instrument theme, and other things I think might sell well. I became interested in selling tea cups and saucers, tea pots, high quality teas, and anything to do with making tea. The idea expanded to hot cocoas and chocolate-covered stirring spoons. The store where I work some of the time is located in a county that allows businesses to offer food sampling. Every couple of months the store owner hosts a special event that includes tea tasting. You might be surprised at the variety of teas and flavors that are on the market these days!

By now you may be asking why, with all the traumatic events, I refer to these times as "The Golden Years." Jerry's prognosis and the other family crises made us more aware than ever how precious our time together is. My experiences have given me strength and knowledge. I have been successful enough to be financially secure. I have seen our children grow and blossom in their own right. I am able to stay active and enjoy the company of family and friends. Sometimes we are placed in different situations. I believe the purpose is to test the strength of our faith and to encourage us to hope for the impossible. In the end, we can watch that faith come to light. I believe I have always been watched over, even in my darkest times. I know this to be true. Look at what I have now: Love from my dear husband, seven children, twenty-three grandchildren, and sixteen great-grandchildren. What more do I need? To my way of thinking, what can be a better start to "Golden Years" than that?

Partners for life!

31. What About Rocky?

It seems only fitting as I approach the end of my book to come full circle and talk more about my life with Rocky. After all, Rocky was the primary reason I was fortunate enough to have Ruth and Joseph raise me as their own. That change in parents greatly impacted my life in more ways than I may ever know. I cannot fully imagine how my life would have been if Connie had raised me. She was a very different person from Ruth, had more children to care for, which meant she'd have had less time for me, and, well, you can probably get the gist of the type of person she was from earlier chapters in this book. Her influence in my life on a full-time basis would likely have made me a different person from what I am today.

Ruth and Joseph always had time for Rocky and me. They took us places and bought us treats when they could. They taught us practical things, like how to cook and keep house. On a deeper level, Mom and Dad impressed on us how to live as honest and compassionate people, to care for each other, and to put family as a priority in our lives.

According to our birth certificates, Rocky is not my biological brother, but, in my mind and heart he IS my brother. When he was young, doctors did not expect him to live much into his thirties. After Mom and Dad died, his care became my sole responsibility, something I took on with no hesitation. I admit there have been a few times that I was frustrated at having this full-time responsibility, but those times have been rare, and it was never about Rocky personally, just the situation. Jerry has been great about incorporating Rocky into our lives, and Linda and her partner Shane are very helpful. We do all the cooking and monitor his glucose level to keep his diabetes under control. For the most part, Rocky can tend to some of his personal hygiene needs. He walks somewhat independently with leg braces and a walker. Someone needs to be close by, however, just in case he falls and can't get up. He attends an adult day school three days a week, using the computers there, makes coffee for the group, and attends social events. He's made friends there, including an occasional girlfriend now and then. At home he likes to spend most of his time in his bedroom coloring in coloring books and watching television. He can tell us all about various celebrities and what movies or shows they've been in. Too bad he can't be on a celebrity trivia game show. I think he'd do very well!

The state pays each month for Rocky's expenses. As a ward of the state, we are visited annually by a state social worker, a county social worker, and the social worker from the adult day school. They make sure that he has his own food, a clean room and clothes, and look at the records of his medical and dental appointments during the year. They talk privately to Rocky and ask questions to make sure he is happy living with Jerry and me. He always tells them he wants to stay right where he is.

Rocky will be eighty-three years old this year! I like to think it's totally been the quality and consistence of our care that has kept him going this long, but I believe there is more to it than that. I believe God has a plan for each of us, and Rocky is fulfilling his personal plan and position in our lives. He remains the sweet, loving person he was when he and I were growing up.

We are happy he is part of our family.

32. The Golden Years Continue ....
More Adventures

A month after the family reunion in Oregon in 2013, we took a trip to Europe with Judy and Alden. We boarded the ship in Amsterdam, The Netherlands, and disembarked in Budapest, Hungary. It was a beautiful cruise on the Blue Danube River. Things do seem to happen for a reason, and this trip was no exception. While on the ship, Jerry wasn't feeling one hundred percent. Leaving nothing to chance, we emailed his doctor to arrange an appointment for as soon as we returned. We enjoyed the trip and celebrated Judy and Alden's fiftieth wedding anniversary with them on board the ship. Once home, Jerry went to the doctor. Tests were ordered and a biopsy done. They found cancer cells in his bladder. We were thinking, 'This can't be possible. Here we go again?' The treatment this time was to surgically scrape the lining of the bladder to remove the tumor. It was outpatient surgery and he came home that day. We anxiously awaited the lab results. They confirmed the tumor was malignant, but the doctor felt they had gotten all of the cancer.

We were already booked on a Fall Colors cruise. Jerry really wanted to go, so we packed up and met Judy and Alden, Leslie and Al, and their friends in Boston.

Jerry's urologist checked him every three months. There were signs of more tumors on the lining of the bladder. Over the next nine months he had two more surgeries to remove lesions or tumors. Every time we got a new diagnosis, it felt like another dip on the roller coaster ride. We could see more than ever that we don't know what our future has in store for us. Going through it all, we became motivated to do whatever might be on Jerry's bucket list while he is still able to enjoy the adventures.

We've looked back at some of our explorations in different countries and at what we have learned about people all over the world. There have been a few incidents that were very unsettling at the time. When on top of the Puerto Plata in the Dominican Republic, our tour bus became stuck on the dirt road out in the middle of what seemed like nowhere. A few poorly dressed children came up to the windows of the bus, holding their hands out, begging for money. I felt sorry for them and started to get my wallet out of my purse. The driver quickly said, in a panicked voice, "Please don't do that, Lady! You'll cause a riot! There are adults hidden in the bushes, watching and waiting. If you give the children money, they will come out and overcome the bus. They might even tip it over." I heeded his warning and closed my purse. It was quite an eye-opening experience.

One year we took a leisure trip to China with Jerry's hiking club. One goal was to climb Yellow Mountain. To get to the top where the hotel was located, we first traveled in a big bus as far as we could go, and then transferred to a mini-bus. The next segment we were put on a gondola that took us to a platform about one mile from the top. From there we climbed stairs that were cut out of the side of the mountain. We climbed for a good hour with our overnight bags. It was well worth all the effort because the views were breath-taking. The sunset was spectacular, and the morning sunrise was priceless. As we were leaving to go back down the mountain, we were told that we would see another area called the Red Lands. That area has been kept a secret because photographers would come from all over the world to capture the beauty. Their photos are so extraordinary that many people suspect they have been enhanced, that this beauty cannot really exist. But it truly does. The soil is layered with so many vibrant colors of the rainbow: purple and red to orange and yellow, mixed with brown and green. With the trees perfectly cut to shape, it looks like a painting - a masterpiece.

The exposure to so many places and cultures that are different from ours has taught us more than about the sites we've seen. We have seen firsthand that people are people, no matter where we go. Mothers all over the world have the same goal to love and protect their children. It is possible to see beauty and compassion if we just look past the stereotypes and the differences to discover our similarities. I believe we can see a little bit of ourselves in each person we meet.

We have been very fortunate to be able to expand our horizons this way! Sometimes we've felt so awestruck, we asked ourselves, "Is this real?" The Pyramids of Egypt, the Great Wall of China, the Hermitage in Russia with its Golden Peacock Clock .... all are so incredibly fascinating to us! On one of our trips to Mexico, I even found out that Joseph's name was in one of the books for that area! I hope to check more into that in the future.

Our most recent trip abroad was with Jerry's brother Al and his wife Leslie, their sister Debbie and her husband Tom, and another couple. We toured ports in the British Isles via cruise ship. It was memorable because of the sites we were able to see, but also because a leg injury Jerry sustained the day before our departure lead to the two of us being ship-bound some of the time. It brought back memories for me of all the days of caring for Mom's leg when it wouldn't heal. She ended up with gangrene and eventual amputation. I knew Jerry's leg would eventually heal, but I felt very uneasy emotionally reliving those moments with Mom. We managed once again to get through this crisis, and spent time playing Scrabble, trivia games, and enjoying decadent cruise ship food while others were touring port cities. We were able to go into some of the ports that didn't require a lot of walking. Over the years we have learned to be flexible. We try to make the best of all situations. That attitude helps to ease stress and makes for a much happier life! I highly recommend it.

Another exciting event for us last year was that Alyssa applied to the court to change her middle and last names. She wanted a new middle name, and to have Jerry listed as her father. We celebrated her adoption, and appreciate that she values the love and attention Jerry gave to her and all my children as they were growing up. He continues to give of himself in their adulthood as well.

Jerry had one more treatment for bladder cancer last year. This one was a bit different and seems to be keeping the cancer cells at bay. It has now been fourteen years since doctors first gave Jerry a two-year prognosis, and Jerry is still with us! Who knows what the future will hold, but we feel very blessed and grateful for advancements in medical technology, paired with the expertise of caring doctors, and God's gift of continuing life.

We have exceptional relationships in our lives and find satisfaction in doing what we can to support family, friends, and our community. We get through each challenge as it comes along. I do believe we are living well in our Golden Years.

I have learned so much over the years! If anyone asks me what my journey has taught me, this would be my answer:

We are stronger than we give ourselves credit for
Learn to trust your instincts and intuition
Get out and experience life
Don't let fear hold you back
Learn from your experiences
Pay attention to messages others offer
We deserve to be treated with respect
Remember to respect and forgive yourself
You are not to blame for being battered or mistreated
You deserve a safe and happy life
Don't give up
Have faith things will work out for the best
Take the time to tell loved ones that you care
Know that you CAN survive

Epilogue

Just as this book was done and ready to go to print, I had an unexpected and enlightening conversation with a member of Dad's family tree. They confirmed some of the stories I'd heard before about my childhood, and they talked about Dad's life in Mexico. As we talked, it was a big surprise to him to hear that I was not really adopted, which is what they had been told. He was also not aware of the letters and money orders Dad had sent to support their family in Mexico after he escaped to the U.S. He told me he might be able to find out the name of my biological father!

Most of the people who could reveal answers to mysteries in my life are already gone. The remaining relatives seem to feel they should not divulge information. They may believe some secrets are not theirs to tell. I respect their attitude of honor and privacy. I am still curious, however, to learn more about the mysteries in our heritage and think it would be good to do away with some of the secrecy in the family.

I'd heard from Rocky years ago that my father was a soldier in 1952. Now I hear that family members did attempt to find him to tell him that he had a child. They think he may have been deployed overseas at the time and were ultimately unable to locate him. As far as they know, he never knew about me.

I've come to realize that at this point in my life, it's really okay if I come to another dead end. Regardless of who one's birth parents are, it is the love from the people who take care of us that counts most. I believe that our destinies are pre-written for us before birth, and that we all have a purpose. I have endured so much and survived. There must be a reason I had to face so many challenges. It will be rewarding for me if sharing my experiences can help other people survive, too. Perhaps this is my purpose.

Appendix

Domestic Violence Resource Guide

National Domestic Violence Hotline	800-799-7233
Nation-wide Resource Center	Call 2-1-1

Cities and Counties have local agencies and programs to help battered women and children. This general list offers key words to help you find them in your area. Check the internet or your local phone book. At home, it might be a good idea to hide your search history on your computer. Or you might use one of the computers with internet access at a library. Clear cell phones of calls and texts to agencies. Doctors, therapists, hospitals, police officers, and social workers, all bound to confidentiality, may be good resources and help guide you to the services that are appropriate for your particular situation. The first step is to take control of your life and seek the help you need. I wish you the best. I believe you *can* do it!

Types of programs and Services:

- 24-hour Crisis Lines
- Emergency Shelter Programs
- Abused Women's Services
- Sexual Assault programs, such as Women Against Rape
- Healthcare clinics
- Mental Health Support
- Counseling services.
- Youth and Family Services Bureaus

Legal Services:

- Family Violence Law Centers
- Local legal aid programs

Bibliography

Berkow, Robert, M.D., Editor-in-Chief, Beers, Mark H., M.D., Associate Editor; Fletcher, Andrew J., M.B., B.Chir., Sr. Assistant Editor, *The Merck Manual of Medical Information, Home Edition,* New York: Pocket Books, 1997.

Chang, Iris, *The Rape of Nanking: The Forgotten Holocaust of World War II*. New York: Basic books, 1997.

Cover: Miller, Valerie, Studio Services, Philadelphia, PA, 2016
www.StudioServices-Design.com
Flowers: Bravoin, "Colorful Flowers." Dreamstime.com
www.dreamstime.com/stock-images-colorful-flowers-image10415484

Public Domain Clip Art Credits: Listed by Chapter number and description of graphic; original artists unknown.

Forward. *Yin and Yang Oriental Mysticism.* http://www.wpclipart.com/religion mythology/symbols/yin_and_yang__Oriental_Mysticism.png.html

1. *Girl with cat.* http://publicdomainvectors.org/en/free-clipart/Victorian-girl-with-kitty-vector-image/31941.html

3. *Heart with Couple.* http://publicdomainvectors.org/en/free-clipart/ Valentine-Vector-Graphics/1906.html

4. *Mother and child.* www.wpclipart.com/people/baby/baby_w_parent/mother_child_flower.png.html

5. *Broken heart.* http://www.wpclipart.com/holiday/valentines/valentine_hearts/broken_heart/broken_heart_pink.png.html

6. *Open book.* http://publicdomainvectors.org/en/free-clipart/Open-book-vector-graphics/12481.html

7. *Mother hugging child.* http://publicdomainvectors.org/en/free-clipart/Image-of-crying-girl-comforted-by-her-mother/35125.html

8. *Party Balloons.* http://www.wpclipart.com/holiday/party/party_balloons.png.html

9. *Eyes.* http://publicdomainvectors.org/en/free-clipart/Vector-clip-art-of-evil-womans-eyes/15358.html

10. *Packed box.* http://publicdomainvectors.org/en/free-clipart/Vector-illustration-of-box-filed-with-household-item/21000.html

11. *Protective hands.* http://publicdomainvectors.org/en/free-clipart/Protecting-hands/36189.

12. *Romantic Couple.* http://www.wpclipart.com/signs_symbol/love/flowers_romance_silhouette.png.html

13. *Valentine candy box with rose.* http://www.wpclipart.com/holiday/valentines/valentine_candy_box_w_rose.png.html

14. *Young housewife.* http://publicdomainvectors.org./en/free-clipart/Vector-image-of-young-housewife/25122.html

15. *Wedding bells.* http://www.wpclipart.com/holiday/wedding/rings/wedding_rings_linked_over_heart.jpg

Wedding cake. http://publicdomainvectors.org/en/free-clipart/Vector-illustration-of-wedding-cake/14522.html

16. *Businessmen High Five, modified by author, June 2016.* http://publicdomain vectors.org/en/free-clipart/Businessmen-high-five-vector-image/2305.html

17. *Family holding hands.* http://publicdomainvectors.org/en/free-clipart/Family/40414.html

18. *Scolding Parent.* http://publicdomainvectors.org/en/free-clipart/Angry-father-vector-illustration/18803.html

19. *Praying hands.* http://publicdomainvectors.org/en/free-clipart/Praying-hands-vector-image/3379.html

20. *Travel documents.* http://publicdomainvectors.org/en/free-clipart/passport-and-ticket-vector/37122.html

21. *Embrace the world.* http://www.wpclipart.com/people/groups/more_the_world.png.html

22. *Floral garland.* http://www.wpclipart.com/plants/flowers/bouquet_basket/flower_and_fruit_festoon.png.html

24. *Girl crying* . http://publicdomainvectors.org/en/ free-clipart/Upset-woman/40348.html

25. *Woman celebrating.* http://www.wpclipart.com/people/female/woman_2/lady_celebrating.png.html

26. *Handshake.* http://publicdomainvectors.org/en/free-clipart/Handshake-vector-illustration/2141.html

27. *Teen shadows.* http://publicdomainvectors.org/en/free-clipart/People-silhouette-vector-drawing/22476.html

28. *Medal of Achievement*. http://publicdomainvectors.org/en/free-clipart/Award-of-achievement-vector-clip-art/19942.html

29. *Chinese House*. http://publicdomainvectors.org/en/free-clipart/Vector-clip-art-of-Chinese-house/29926.html

30. *Swans*. www.wpclipart.com/animals/birds/S/swan/Swan_2/Whooper_Swans_on_lake.jpg.html

31. *Smiley face*. http://www.wpclipart.com/smiley/simple _ smiley/smiley_button/smiley_button_pink.png.html

32. *Sunrise over rolling hills*. http://www.wpclipart.com/scenic/wallpaper/sunset/sunrise_over_rolling_hills.jpg.html

Made in the USA
Las Vegas, NV
09 January 2022

40754820R00134